Transforming
A Wasted Land

A Future for Namibia 2
Agriculture

Transforming
A Wasted Land

Richard Moorsom

The Catholic Institute for International Relations

First published in November 1982 by
Catholic Institute for International Relations, 22 Coleman Fields, London
N1 7AF

©Richard Moorsom 1982
ISBN 0 904393 85 2

Moorsom, Richard
  Agriculture. (A Future for Namibia; 2)
  1. Agriculture — Economic aspects — Namibia
  I. Title   II. Series
  338.1'09688   HD2134

Copies available by post from CIIR. Trade distribution to bookshops and
library supplies by Third World Publications Ltd, 151 Stratford Road,
Birmingham B11 1RD, Tel. 021-773 6572.

Printed by the Russell Press Ltd, Bertrand Russell House, Nottingham
(UK).

Design by Jan Brown 01-837 5296.

Contents

Tables

Tables in Appendix

Maps

Map 1 Namibia

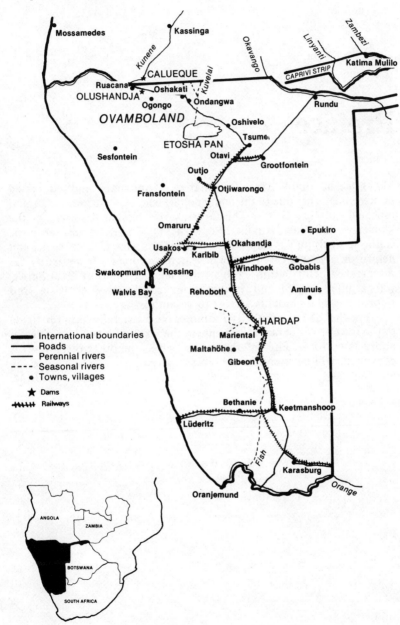

Preface

My grateful thanks for information, comments and suggested improvements are due to the many people who read various drafts and especially to Reg Green. The Overseas Development Group at the University of East Anglia, Norwich, DEFA Research, and the Catholic Institute for International Relations were also generous and helpful in giving access to their research resources. However, by far the greatest contribution to this study has been that of Paul Spray, whose input of factual information, constructive criticism and rigorous editing amounts almost to co-authorship.

For the sake of simplicity footnotes have generally been restricted to the sources of factual statements in the text and have been given in abbreviated form. Full references, as well as the other main sources consulted, will be found in the bibiography.

R.M.

1 Introduction

Namibia is today the last surviving remnant in Africa of the old European colonial empires. Colonised by Germany at the turn of the century, after the First World War it was passed under League of Nations mandate to South Africa, then within the British imperial sphere. In 1966, after 20 years of fruitless efforts to persuade South Africa to allow the Namibian people to exercise their right to self-determination, the UN General Assembly revoked the mandate. Sixteen years later, South Africa remains in illegal colonial occupation, in defiance both of pressure from its own Western allies and of the growing strength of the liberation movement SWAPO (the South West African People's Organisation of Namibia).

This study has two principal objectives: to present an up-to-date outline analysis of Namibia's agriculture and the forces that have shaped it during the colonial epoch; and to discuss alternative paths of rural development open to a newly independent Namibian government. Two thirds of the population live in the rural areas, depending partly or wholly on agriculture for their income. About 90% spend part of their lives on the land, particularly in childhood and old age. The future of agriculture is therefore of major importance to the future of Namibia.

Three structural factors are central to agriculture in Namibia. Firstly, as in South Africa, the most productive land has been parcelled out to subsidised settler farmers, and the remnants of the pre-colonial black peasantry confined to over-crowded reserves. From these islands of poverty and unemployment, sheer necessity has driven succeeding generations of men from peasant householders into the endless circuit of short-term labour migration. It is on this foundation of cheap and regimented labour that the prosperity of the colonial capitalist economy has been built. Secondly, agriculture has been honed to the requirements of industrial South Africa, in particular its

9

need of red meat supplies for its cities, and export markets for its manufacturers and cereal and dairy farmers. Thirdly, the effects of this pattern of colonial exploitation have been sharpened by a harsh natural environment, the driest south of the Sahara, which confines non-irrigated cultivation to small areas in the north, and limits pasture use in the centre and south to very low densities of livestock.

There has hitherto been little public debate inside Namibia on development policy, beyond a dogmatic insistence by South Africa's spokesmen and political clients on the virtues of laissez-faire capitalism and in particular of small business enterprise. For the liberation movement and most black Namibians, the struggle for national liberation and surviving the terrors of South African military repression are the immediate and urgent priorities. The lack of open discussion has been exacerbated by South African education policy in Namibia, which has denied the country its own university and stifled policy-oriented research. As a result, many of the available studies of the Namibian economy and agricultural sector have been published abroad, largely by Western aid agencies and research institutes. More importantly, both the UN Institute for Namibia and the FAO, reinforced by the work of sympathetic scholars, have initiated research on transitional planning.

Any agrarian reform designed to promote social justice and to fulfil basic human needs will face severe obstacles — political, economic and environmental. More than four-fifths of currently viable farmland is owned by white ranchers, most of them strongly hostile to decolonisation under any conditions. Should large numbers of settlers leave, a simple reversion of their ranches to subsistence farming, as has happened to varying degrees in Kenya and Zimbabwe, would not be a complete answer given present population levels, because only in a few areas and in years of above normal rainfall is it possible to grow staple grains. The peasant areas of the far north are already grossly overcrowded. Only careful planning and considerable infrastructural investment will enable them to provide adequately for their populations.

At the threshold of independence, therefore, there is likely to be little room for compromise between two radically opposed alternatives: on the one hand, a continuation of the present expensive and highly inegalitarian private enterprise ranching system in the interests of maintaining high levels of agricultural exports; on the other, comprehensive agrarian reform embracing both the commercial and peasant sectors.

2 The Context

2.1 Geography and Natural Environment

Namibia is a vast, wedge-shaped territory over three times the size of the UK and two-thirds the size of South Africa itself. A high plateau, lying mostly at an altitude of between 1 250 and 1 750m, is faced in the west by an escarpment 80 to 130km inland from the coast (Map 2). The escarpment and the northwestern uplands (the Kaokoveld) are mountainous, and there are substantial ranges in the centre and south east; otherwise the terrain is fairly flat. To the east and north the plateau descends gradually into the flat Kalahari sands, and this demarcates the basic division of soils in Namibia between relatively good quality 'hardveld' on the plateau, and the poorer 'sandveld', which is not only less fertile but also absorbs rainfall quickly so that surface water disappears very early in the dry season.

Namibia has the driest climate in Africa south of the Sahara, and it is rainfall which defines the main land use zones: the coastal desert; the small-stock zone; a transitional zone; the large-stock zone; and the mixed farming zone (Map 3). Along the coastal strip the Namib desert, though cool and foggy for much of the year, receives almost no rain. The only concentrations of vegetation to be found among its desolate sand dunes and rocky outcrops lie along the sandy beds of underground rivers. Towards the escarpment the temperature increases sharply and occasional summer showers bring on short-lived flushes of grass which provide valuable temporary grazing.

In the interior, average annual rainfall increases from south to north. Below 250mm the pasture is too sparse for cattle and this therefore demarcates the second land-use area, the small-stock zone. It embraces the whole of the plateau hardveld south of Rehoboth, together with minor pockets of sandveld — 30% of the land area of Namibia. The soil is generally thin and poor, but over much of the plateau the sparse cover of grass tussocks and low woody shrubs

11

Map 2   Relief and Rainfall

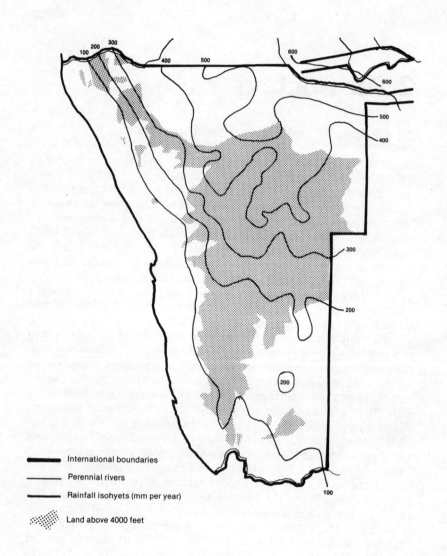

International boundaries

Perennial rivers

Rainfall isohyets (mm per year)

Land above 4000 feet

Map 3   Land Use Zones

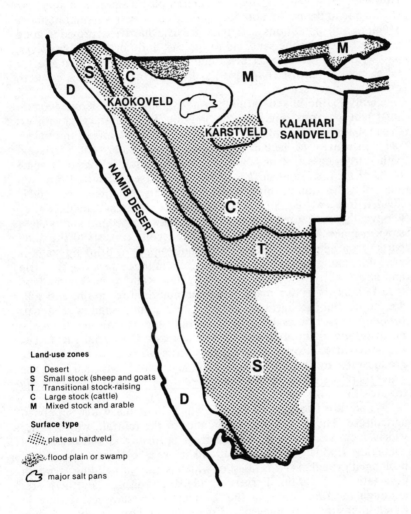

Land-use zones

D   Desert
S   Small stock (sheep and goats
T   Transitional stock-raising
C   Large stock (cattle)
M   Mixed stock and arable

Surface type

plateau hardveld

flood plain or swamp

major salt pans

provides good browse for sheep and goats.

Between the large and small-stock zones, lies a transitional belt, receiving between 250mm and 350mm of rain, where limited numbers of cattle can be raised, but sheep and goats remain in a majority. However, cattle generally require a denser pasture and the main large-stock zone in the centre and north of the country has a rainfall above 350mm. Soil conditions subdivide it. The hardveld provides good pasture for cattle; the sandveld to the east and north west, however, has serious mineral deficiencies and high salinity, which make for lower quality pasture, and also has little surface water for cattle to drink in the dry season.

Only in the mixed farming zone is rainfall, at above 500mm, sufficient for crops as well as stock-rearing. Even so, the area with less than 550mm is marginal for grain crops. Three-quarters of the zone is today little used, for lack of year-round surface water — it is sandveld with fairly dense tree and bush cover. The result is that only some 6.5% of the total land surface of Namibia is used for mixed farming, and only a fraction of this is under crops at any one time. This land is divided into two equal areas. The first is the Otavi highlands, or karstveld[1], where good soil and rainfall between 500mm and 600mm support maize, fruit and vegetables. The second consists of the small parts of the sandveld where a year-round supply of drinking water is available: along the Okavango river valley, in the eastern Caprivi Strip and above all on the Ovambo flood plain. Rainfall in Ovamboland (400-550mm) is in fact marginal to sub-marginal for grain, and soils are poor, but an intricate network of broad, shallow channels (*oshana*) redistributes both local rainfall and floodwater from the north (*efundja*), brought chiefly by the seasonal Kuvelai River. The accumulated rainwater is prevented from mixing with the saline groundwater by an impervious subsoil layer close to the surface. The water therefore takes months to evaporate or filter through the *oshana* towards the Etosha Pan.

There are two general factors which limit the water supply to agriculture. The first is the unreliability of the rainfall, which varies widely from year to year, causing frequent droughts and occasional damaging floods. There is a broad 15-year cycle of severe and prolonged droughts — the latest of which is only just ending — which devastate both grain harvests and stock-raising. Furthermore, although the rain comes in the form of heavy showers of roughly equal intensity, it is unevenly distributed in both space and time through the rainy season. Early rains followed by a dry six to eight

---

1. The karstveld is a dolomite/limestone formation which absorbs rainwater rapidly and therefore retains a good reserve of groundwater.

weeks at the height of the tropical summer heat may do as much damage to growing crops and annual grasses as a full-scale drought. Likewise, the tracks of a few big showers may make the difference between normality for one locality and drought for its neighbour, a risk which increases as average rainfall becomes scantier. In the far south, where the entire annual rainfall usually comes from a handful of showers scattered over a period of perhaps three or four months, the line between sufficiency and unbroken drought is very much a hit and miss affair. Even in Ovamboland it has been estimated that drought or damaging flood has affected part or the whole of the region in 63 years out of 105.[2]

The second general constraint is the scarcity of surface drinking water for people and animals. Nowhere except in the far north for a brief two to three months at the height of the rainy season does the rainfall come near to matching the rate of evaporation and plant transpiration. As a result, nearly all the rainwater returns to the atmosphere soon after falling and watercourses flow for only a few weeks or at best several months — the only permanently flowing rivers originate outside the country and form its northern and southern boundaries.

Under these conditions the hardveld is much better provided than the sandveld. Here many of the streams retain their water below the surface of their sandy beds throughout the year. Groundwater re-emerges in scattered springs and waterholes or may be extracted through boreholes. In the sandveld, however, only the largest watercourses (*omuramba*) and pans retain their water throughout the dry winter. Furthermore, because little rainwater penetrates more than 7 metres deep, any groundwater is often limited in quantity, at great depths in the rock sub-strata, and sometimes saline. Both stock-raising and arable farming are therefore usually more productive and secure in the plateau hardveld than in their equivalent rainfall zones on the sandveld. Throughout the country, however, the vegetation and soils are fragile and vulnerable to over-exploitation: careful management of natural resources has always been and remains an essential condition of long-term agricultural productivity, whether with stock or with crops.

2.2 Pre-colonial Agriculture

Before the intrusion of colonialism, the inhabitants of what is now

---

2. During the period 1868-1972 (Moorsom 1977, p.57 and sources cited, *ibid.*, note 57 thereat).

Namibia practised varied and sophisticated forms of land-use. Their importance today stems not merely from the fact that the colonisers have permitted remnants of pre-colonial agriculture to survive in the reserves, albeit in a severely deformed state, but also from the centuries of accumulated skill and experience which, despite everything, have been passed down to the present generation of peasant farmers. Moreover, the pre-colonial traditions of cooperation and sharing contrast sharply with the authoritarian, exploitative methods of settler farming and will remain highly relevant to the principles and objectives of rural development under a post-independence Namibian government.

Until the early 19th century Namibia was largely isolated from the world-wide expansion of European commerce and empire-building by the formidable barrier of the Namib desert. Given the limitations of a stone- or iron-age technology, agricultural techniques were well developed and ecologically adapted. Hunting birds and animals and collecting fruits, leaves and roots made an important contribution to food and medicinal requirements. For the San hunter-gatherer bands in the dry sandveld these were the sole sources of subsistence, and required considerable bushcraft skills, intimate local knowledge and great mobility over wide areas. In the small-stock zone their importance was almost as great. Highly organised hunting techniques were developed, using fire, open-pit traps or dogs. In addition, in the far north fruit trees were carefully preserved and forest areas protected. Here too, fresh-water fish in the permanent rivers and the seasonal *efundja* contributed a valuable source of protein.

Wherever access to a winter water supply permitted, stock-raising was widely practised: sheep, goats and a few cattle in the small-stock zone, cattle alone on the northern hardveld, and both in the far north, although here serious stock diseases and tropical parasites were endemic and the indigenous breeds were smaller in size. On the plateau hardveld, the long distances between waterholes and the scarcity of winter water supplies were more powerful factors in limiting stock numbers than the carrying capacity of the pasture itself. Constant mobility in search of pasture and water was an essential way of coping with the intermittence and irregular distribution of the rainfall. These conditions required a nomadic way of life with no permanent settlements except at a few favoured water holes. In the far north, on the other hand, even in winter the water supply was usually adequate. During the crop season, cattle were dispatched to temporary posts in the surrounding sandveld and along the uninhabited sections of the permanent rivers to the north, returning to graze the field stubble after harvest and the winter grasses in the dried-out *oshana* beds and the narrow floodplain of the Okavango. Field agriculture was much more limited in extent, even where the average rainfall was sufficient, but in the few areas where the winter water supply was adequate a fairly dense agricultural settlement arose. Crops were grown extensively along the margins of the *oshana*. To overcome the low soil fertility and waterlogged conditions during the rainy season, the sandy topsoil was worked with hoes into small mounds (about 50cm high), which were then directly manured and planted by hand. The pasturing of cattle in harvest stubble and the frequent rotation of the site of the stockaded homestead complex within its field area also made important contributions to the long-term build-up of soil fertility. The principal crops were drought-resistant grains, principally millet (*mahangu*) and to a lesser extent sorghum, complemented by a range of beans, nuts and vegetables. Fleshy varieties such as melons and pumpkins could be invaluable in time of drought. Similar crops were grown on the narrow terraces of the Okavango Valley, whose slightly better drainage, soil fertility and rainfall gave a limited degree of insurance against drought and floods. Further east, in what is now the eastern Caprivi Strip, the higher rainfall (600mm) made possible the cultivation of maize at some distance from the swampy margins of the Zambezi and its tributaries. In the rest of Namibia, the only cultivation was in small garden plots, usually near springs in the northern and north western hardveld.

These systems were, however, vulnerable. Prolonged or severe drought decimated herds both through starvation and through lack of drinking water, and in the far north devastated grain crops as well. The impact of severe drought was if anything most catastrophic in the densely populated Ovambo floodplain, where crop failure and the rapid drying up of surface water confronted both people and animals with combined water and food starvation. It is possible that as many as a quarter of the Ovambo population of about 160,000 died in the great famine of 1915 and the influenza epidemic which struck three years later.[3]

Social organisation was strongly influenced by the form of land use. San (Bushmen) hunting bands were not normally more than 30 strong, and clans of Nama and Damara small-stock herders ranged from a few score to a couple of thousand. Each distinct group was politically autonomous and controlled a large economic zone with fluctuating boundaries, within which it ranged widely. For them as for the Herero cattle-pastoralists, who were politically decentralised but occupied a common economic zone, land was an open communal

---

3.   Including that part of pre-colonial Ovamboland now in Angola. References to
      Ovamboland after 1915 indicate only the southern half now within Namibia.

resource with no individual use-rights.

By contrast, in the *oshana* floodplain the Ovambo were concentrated in about a dozen clusters of continuous, permanent and dense settlement, separated by strips of uninhabited woodland. Within each, the pattern of settlement was dispersed, with no villages as such. Each homestead was located in the midst of its fields, to which the household head held a lifetime use-right. The clusters, each of which was politically independent, ranged in size from as little as a thousand in the drier far west to 60-80 000 in the largest, Ukwanyama, which was situated in the better-watered north-east and also astride the Kuvelai River. Each cluster controlled an economic zone larger than its immediate area of settlement, including the surrounding woodland and wide areas of distant sandveld pasture. The two largest clusters, Ukwanyama and Ondonga, also controlled the sources of their metal ores, copper from Otavi and iron from Kassinga, 250km to the south and north respectively. The narrow strip of settlement along the Okavango valley was similarly organised. Only near the Zambezi in the east was the more usual central African pattern of village settlement the general rule.

Throughout pre-colonial Namibia political authority was decentralised. Only in the larger of the Ovambo and Okavango clusters had hereditary rulers emerged who controlled the allocation of land through appointed district administrators, and levied labour, and occasionally cattle, taxes on their subjects. At the same time the rulers recruited expert advisers and performed important agricultural functions, in particular the maintenance of dry-season wells, the preservation of fruit trees, setting the start of the planting season (which was notoriously difficult to judge), and supervising the annual cattle drive. Nevertheless, even in the most powerful Ovambo kingdoms, as elsewhere throughout the region, the clan structure provided a strong and durable social framework and an alternative, decentralised mode of political organisation. Through it, complex mechanisms of stock loan and inheritance operated within all stock-raising societies, redistributing stock socially and geographically through wide networks of relatives and clients. By this means, permanent concentrations of stock in the hands of wealthy owners were usually prevented.

The dispersal of stock also helped to spread losses in times of drought and war. In order to compensate for a run of bad harvests, Ovambo households built large basketwork containers capable of storing up to five years' grain supply. They protected the grain from insects, rodents and damage by rot by treating it with ash, raising the basket on poles, and lining it with clay and adding a roof. In addition cooperative work practices were widely established, particularly at the local level. Groups of families collaborated in hunting, in organising stock movements, in fishing, and in heavy field labour such as clearing the ground and gathering in the harvest.

Redistributive social forces, the decentralisation of political authority and the environmental barriers to the accumulation of personal wealth all tended to limit concentrations of economic and political power. In none of the four principal pre-colonial societies — hunter-gatherers, small-stock herders, cattle pastoralists and mixed stock and arable farmers — were conquered or subordinate social groups a significant proportion of the population. Relations of clientship tended to be reciprocal: hunter-gatherers, for instance, might join groups of herders at difficult times of year, or perform specialised tasks such as mining for payment in kind. Where conflicts arose between practitioners of different modes of land-use — between hunters and cattle-herders over the burning of pasture, or between large- and small-stock herders over scarce pasture and water in time of drought — it was usually local and shortlived. On the other hand, the whole region was united by ties of trade in which implements manufactured from iron and copper, chiefly by Ovambo smiths, were among the principal items of exchange. Many of the traders were also artisans who made and repaired metal artefacts as they travelled. The extent of interdependence is illustrated by one of the principal chains of supply, in which copper ore mined at Otavi by local San was worked by Ovambo smiths and then traded for cattle over much of present-day Namibia and into Botswana.

The most systematic inequality in pre-colonial peasant society lay between men and women. In all groups a division of labour operated in which most productive tasks were allocated according to sex. Hunting and cattle-herding, mobile activities which provided much of the high-protein food requirements, were exclusive male preserves; gathering, field cultivation and fishing were done predominantly by women. Although children began to participate in production well before puberty and were socialised and trained by adults of their own sex, early child-rearing was almost exclusively the responsibility of women, as was the preparation of food for male household members. The division of labour was least unequal in the San hunting bands, whose skills and tasks were fairly evenly apportioned. In the pastoral societies, the exclusion of women from hunting and most stock-raising severely limited their participation in production and confined them to tasks near the home.

Amongst the Ovambo, women, as the chief cultivators and fishers, played a more equal part and also undertook much of the craftwork and organised the herding of goats and poultry. However, men were the heads of household in whom use-rights to the family fields were vested, and so male authority was still predominant. Polygamy was used by men to acquire additional field and domestic labour. As amongst the stock-farmers, no woman could choose a way of life independent of marriage or of subordinate status in a male-run household. Women nevertheless possessed considerable managerial autonomy in field and household labour, and had the right to the produce of private plots of their own. In both stock-keeping and cultivating societies, men held a monopoly of political and military power as well as overall control of production and the distribution of its proceeds.

Notwithstanding its simple technology, its vulnerability to prolonged drought and the subordinate position of women, pre-colonial agriculture thus contained important positive features. These included a sophisticated adaptation to a difficult local environment, social mechanisms for mutual support and the redistribution of accumulated wealth, and cooperative work methods.

Well before German colonisation in the 1890s pre-colonial societies in Namibia were severely disrupted by the ripple effects of colonial expansion in South Africa and by the intrusion of European commerce. Between 1800 and 1870, waves of refugees arrived from South Africa, overcrowding the small-stock zone and generating increasingly desperate competition for pasture and water-holes. From the 1840s onward, white traders crisscrossed the interior, building up consumer demand for imported goods and extending credit for which they demanded payment in cattle at advantageous terms. Cattle-raiding, especially by those with insufficient cattle of their own, was encouraged. Amongst the stock farmers of the plateau hardveld, the resulting disunity and conflict led to spiralling expenditure on weapons, depletion of herds (especially sheep and goats in the south), growing numbers of impoverished refugees and dependants, and increasingly authoritarian relationships between ruler and ruled. In Ovamboland the kings were forced to step up the cattle tax on their subjects in order to pay for imported arms for defence against the Portuguese and the Germans. By the end of the 19th century stock-raising was under serious pressure throughout the region and the people had been politically divided by economic competition, easing the way for the colonial invasion.

3 The Agriculture of Theft

Both the German (1884-1915) and the South African (1915 onwards) colonial regimes wanted Namibia for minerals, and for white settler farmers. Both aims required wholesale seizure of land, thereby reducing the area available to peasant production and forcing the dispossessed to become wage labourers. As Paul Rohrbach, Commissioner for Settlement in South West Africa between 1903 and 1906, succinctly expressed it:[1]

> The decision to colonise in Southern Africa means nothing else than that the native tribes must withdraw from the lands on which they have pastured their cattle and so let the white man pasture his cattle on these self-same lands. If the moral rights of this standpoint are questioned, the answer is that for people of the cultural standard of the South African natives, the loss of their free natural barbarism and the development of a class of workers in the service of and dependent on whites is above all a law of survival of the highest order.

At first, the Germans pursued their objectives not by full-scale conquest but by selective dispossession of some groups and 'protection treaties' with the rest. Between 1894 and 1904, fully backed by the colonial police and courts, settlers pushed into communal land on the plateau hardveld. The herds, already severely reduced by the rinderpest epidemic of 1897, were further depleted by the demands of traders insisting on taking cattle in settlement of their credit. In desperation, in 1904 the Herero, Damara and Nama rose against the German colonial regime, with the active support of the Ovambo in the north. The German response was a ruthless campaign of genocide, which killed some 60% of the black population of the

---

1.   Quoted in SWAPO 1981, p.17.

Figure 1

Land Distribution between Peasants and Commercial Farming, 1982 (by Land Use Zones)

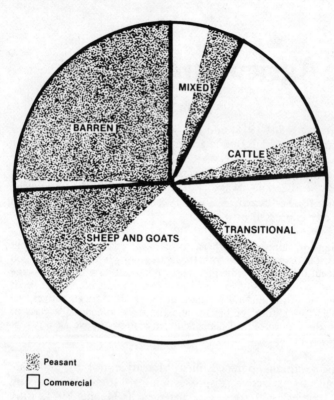

Peasant

Commercial

For definition of land use zones, see text and map.

Rehoboth Gebiet included in peasant sector.

Source: Appendix Table A4

Map 4   Land Distribution: Population and Bantustans

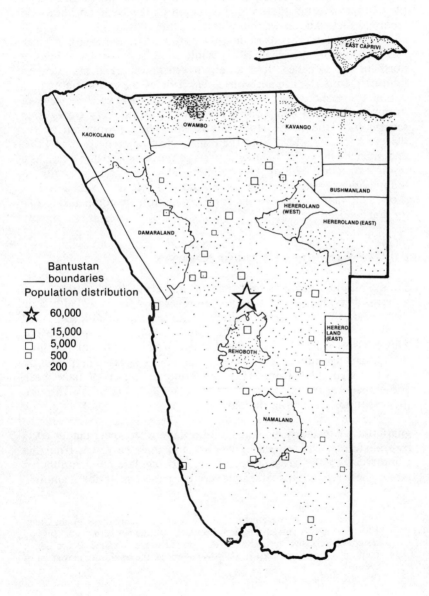

EAST CAPRIVI

KAOKOLAND

OWAMBO

KAVANGO

BUSHMANLAND

DAMARALAND

HEREROLAND (WEST)

HEREROLAND (EAST)

Bantustan
boundaries
Population distribution

☆ 60,000
☐ 15,000
☐ 5,000
☐ 500
• 200

REHOBOTH

HERERO LAND (EAST)

NAMALAND

23

plateau hardveld and nearly all their livestock. Thereafter the regime expropriated nearly all communal land on the hardveld except for the Rehoboth Gebiet, whose inhabitants had not joined the uprising, and began distributing it to white settlers. Only the far north escaped — the Germans feared the military strength of the Ovambo kings and regarded their land as less suitable for white settlement.

This general dispensation was confirmed by the South African regime which took over in 1915. While white settlement was banned north of the so called 'Red Line',[2] which had marked the northern limit of German police authority, very little of the expropriated land within the Police Zone was returned. Map 4 shows the extent of dispossession, and comparison with Map 3 shows very clearly that settlers took the prime stock-raising land. The proportion of the plateau hardveld allocated to the reserves is now no more than 12%, and much of that is in the poorer parts of the dry south and west. As a result less than a fifth of the currently viable farmland in Namibia is today under peasant occupation (Fig.1 and Table A4). Yet, as Map 4 shows, the vast majority of the rural population are compelled to live on that land.

3.1 The Creation of Labour Reserves

Today, although three to four times as numerous as the settler farms in terms of population, the peasant reserves contribute probably little more than 5% of total agricultural sales and, according to a 1977 estimate,[3] only about 13% of the value of agricultural production. This contrast is by no means the simple consequence of colonial land theft, nor is agriculture in the reserves merely a stagnated perpetuation of its pre-colonial forms. On the contrary, reserves have been consciously turned to the needs of the commercial economy through the institution of migrant labour.

The colonial administration had three main objectives: to guarantee a constantly available pool of labour; to lower labour costs by transferring the burden of welfare and unemployment from the commercial to the peasant sector; and to regulate competition for labour between groups of employers of greatly differing economic

---

2. The 'Red Line', whose precise course was altered many times by the South Africans, cuts off part of northern 'Damaraland', the northern bantustans and eastern 'Hereroland' from the rest of Namibia — the so-called 'Police Zone'. Today it is fenced and used as a barrier to prevent the southward movement of livestock.
3. Green & Kiljunen 1981, Table 15.

strengths. To these ends an interrelated land and labour policy was developed. In the reserves, communal land tenure was enforced, slowing the emergence of landlessness by giving every household the right of access to the land. Large accumulations of stock were also obstructed — although not completely prevented — in the north by barring access to markets, and in the centre/south by taxing stock and limiting herd sizes. Thus peasant households were to retain a stake in agricultural production but, given the shortage of land, it would be a stake inadequate for self-sufficiency. People would therefore have to leave to find work. At the same time, 'influx control' laws allowed inhabitants to leave the reserves only as short-term migrant labourers. For employers, this had the advantage that wages did not have to cover the needs of workers' families and so could be kept low. For workers, the result was to separate them from their families, deny them the right to settle permanently in the so-called 'white' area, and force them to return to the reserves when sick, disabled, retired, unemployed, or victimised by employers, officials or the courts.

The Germans turned the circumstances of conquest to their advantage. Having killed off the majority of the inhabitants of the Police Zone between 1904 and 1907, they were suddenly faced with a growing shortage of labour for the new Tsumeb copper mine, the diamond fields south of Lüderitz and the railway construction programme. In a tacit compromise with the Ovambo kings, the colonial regime recognised their autonomy in return for the dispatch of large numbers of short-term contract labourers. Cattle disease, the cattle tax and political disruption had already eroded the position of the male cattle-herders in Ovambo economic life. The number of labour migrants rose rapidly, reaching 10 000 per year by 1910.

The South Africans formalised this arrangement by creating a two-tier system of reserves. Those in the Police Zone — small, fragmented, situated on inferior land on the edges of the hardveld and containing less than 15% of the total peasant population — were to provide labour for the white farms. The northern reserves, however, with 85% of the population — above all Ovamboland — were regarded as the chief suppliers of migrant labour. Although it had been cut in two by the boundary with Angola, Ovamboland had not suffered the severity of land theft and devastation of the stock-farming south, and the peasant economy was still substantially intact. Nevertheless it was no longer self-sufficient, and labour migration was from the outset an economic necessity. Table 1 shows the rising population in the reserves, and the corresponding flow of migrant labour. The contract labour system, imposed on these reserves by the South Africans in the 1920s, was to be the foundation of the white colonisers' prosperity.

25

Table 1

The Rural Black Population in the Reserves, 1925-70

		1925	1939	1960¹	1970	1970 % of total	1970 Resident	1970 Migrant workers as proportion of rural men (%)
		(000s)	(000s)	(000s)	(000s)		(000s)	
Police Zone	Small-stock reserves²	7.1	11.1	13.8	21.9	4.7	20.1	30
	Large-stock reserves³	4.6	13.9	15.8	21.3	4.5	20.4	16
	Total	*11.7*	*25.0*	*29.6*	*43.2*	*9.2*	*40.5*	*25*
Northern Zone	Kaokoveld	(4)	6	9	12.4	2.6	12.2	7
	Ovamboland	(95)	130	231	332	70.6	290	48
	Okavango	(16)	20	28	55.3	11.8	52.3	21
	East Caprivi Strip	(10)	13	16	26.7	5.7	25.5	18
	Total	*(125)*	*179*	*284*	*426*	*90.7*	*380*	*44*
All reserves	Total	(137)	204	314	470	100	421	36

All figures are approximate and probably substantially understated; those in brackets are rough estimates. Except for the final column of 1970 ('resident'), they include migrant workers outside the reserves.

Notes
1. 1960/61 for the Police Zone.
2. Berseba, Tses, Bondelswarts, Warmbad, Soromas, Gibeon, Neuhof, Hoachanas, Otjimbingwe, Otjohorongo, Okombahe, Fransfontein; Rehoboth Gebiet excluded because not communal tenure. Additions of marginal grazing land under the bantustan programme may partly account for the very high 1960-70 growth rate of 4.7% per annum.
3. Otjituuo, Waterberg East, Eastern, Epukiro, Aminuis, Ovitoto.

Sources
SWA Administrator, *Annual Reports* 1925 & 1939; SWA Scientific Society 1965, p.96; Census 1921, 1960, 1970.

The Police Zone reserves

In the centre/south (the so-called Police Zone) the lives of the inhabitants of the remaining reserves were subordinated to the needs of the white settler farming community. Land seizure was such that then, as now, less than a fifth of the black population of the Police Zone actually lived in the reserves themselves: the rest were on the new settler farms or in the towns. The reserves served as a safety valve, firstly as a supplementary source of labour, secondly as a dumping-ground for sick, elderly or redundant workers. Thirdly, since many white farmers allowed black workers to accumulate small herds of their own in lieu of cash wages, the reserves acted as depositories to which workers could transfer the stock which represented their savings. Such a safety valve proved very useful to the white settlers when in times of drought or depression they wanted to reduce their workforce or take over the grazing for their own animals.

Despite South African neglect, and although confined to a fraction of their former territories or pushed into the desert margins, not all the black pastoralists of the Police Zone succumbed to the logic of migrant labour. Some managed to move their families to town in defiance of the law. Others re-invested their savings from wages and rebuilt a modified agriculture, with significant sales of cattle, milk and karakul.

Self-sufficiency nevertheless remained a remote prospect for all but the largest stock owners. In Waterberg East in 1957 only 8% of resident men had more than fifty head of cattle, and 20% none at all; in Aminuis 30% had none.[4] The small and fragmented area of the 18 Police Zone reserves and the inferior quality of their pasture and water supply anyway placed severe restrictions on the gross volume of their output. Under these conditions labour migration was from the start a necessity, as a means both of survival and of accumulating savings. The available rough population estimates suggest that between 1925 and 1955 at least 15-25% of resident adult males — in practice probably many more — were absent at any one time, the periods varying from a few months to several years at a time.

The northern reserves

In the reserves north of the Red Line the South African administration followed the German example, designating them the chief suppliers of migrant labour to the mines and the state and excluding white settlement. Politically, in contrast to its policy in the central/southern reserves, which it administered directly, South Africa preferred 'indirect rule', coopting some of the pre-colonial rulers as paid officials under the close supervision of a skeleton white staff.

4.   These are reserves in the west of present-day 'Hereroland'.

Economically, instead of allowing licensed white traders and sales of peasant produce, it sealed off the region altogether from the commercial economy, leaving labour migration as the only way of earning a cash income. The state went to considerable lengths to isolate northern agriculture: a total ban was imposed on the southward movement of cattle, sales of produce outside the reserves were prevented, and until the 1960s only three stores, owned by the semi-official labour recruiting agency SWANLA (the South West African Native Labour Association), were licensed in the entire north. Opportunities for earning cash within the reserves were virtually non-existent; the only legal way of earning it outside was as a short-term migrant labourer contracted to SWANLA.

The fragile ecology of the floodplain and the lack of savings precluded major changes in agricultural technology or methods (in contrast to the peasant areas of southeastern Africa, for instance, where trade led to the widespread adoption of the plough and of new crops). However, there was one important change: the principal pre-colonial control on rising population was removed. The earnings of contract workers and South African organisation of district grain stores (supplied by a grain tax and relief imports) enabled people to survive periodic famine. By 1970 the population had expanded more than threefold within half a century.

The rising population required land, and by the 1970s the whole of the relatively well-watered *oshana* zone was densely settled — at the expense of spare grazing, hunting and wood (for building and fuel). As many as 60 000 — over a fifth of the resident population in 1970 — had moved to the east and south-east of the *oshana* zone, an area with weak and unreliable seasonal streams and served in 1974 by at most 24 boreholes and 25 small reservoirs.[5] As the scarcity of land intensified, agriculture became increasingly precarious. Official estimates suggest a tripling in the total number of cattle and goats between the 1930s and 1970s. At the same time, pasture land was reduced both by cultivation and by the Angolan border, which cut off much of the pre-colonial summer grazing especially after it was fenced in the 1950s. Heavy mortality during drought was inevitable, and stock-raising became an increasingly risky process.

In the most crowded district of central Ukwanyama the stocking ratio was already down to under 2ha per head of cattle by 1955, and even less if non-grazing and arable land is excluded — far below the safe carrying capacity of the pasture. Indeed, in the early 1970s, 80% of the pasture in this area was reported 'almost totally destroyed'.[6] It

---

5. Derived from Stellenbosch 1978, figs 3.1 and 4.1.
6. Stellenbosch 1978, Table 2.12, based on Opperman, undated.

is no surprise, then, that in the drought between 1955 and 1959, by no means the driest period on record, the district of Ukwanyama lost more than half its total stock.[7] Overall, average cattle ownership has dropped over the last 25 years. In addition, in conditions of increasingly desperate pasture shortage, inequalities in cattle ownership have become marked. A 1968 survey of a sample of contract workers found that three-quarters of their households in the northern reserves held 10 or less cattle, while only a tenth held 25 or more.[8]

Arable agriculture also came under increasingly severe pressure. Official figures suggest that per capita grain output, barely adequate at 2½ bags per person in 1957 (1 bag = 90 kg), dropped by a third within the space of 15 years, despite a probable increase in gross volume.[9] While the accuracy of official figures may be doubted, they demonstrate the reality of land shortage and declining per capita returns. This is in sharp contrast to the South African claim, echoed uncritically in some recent independent studies, that Ovamboland is self-sufficient in grain in normal rainfall years. Indeed, a 1974 South African survey estimated that 34% of rural Ovambo cash expenditure went to buy food. Conversely, agricultural production made up only a third of their total income — the rest had to come from elsewhere.[10]

The need for a cash income, reinforced after the mid-1930s by the growing inadequacy of subsistence production, forced ever larger numbers of Ovambo to join the migrant labour circuit. By the 1950s 30-35% of Ovambo men were away on contract at any one time and by 1970 as many as 45%, a massive withdrawal of adult labour from the peasant agricultural cycle. Over the past 25 years, as rural impoverishment has deepened, the wages of contract workers have been the only means of averting mass starvation during drought. When the harvest failed in 1959, the government sent in 100 000 bags of relief maize, not all of which would have been free. Ovambos in and outside Ovamboland bought another 60 000 bags themselves, costing the equivalent at that time of at least two to three months' wages for a contract worker.[11] Other areas and forms of peasant agriculture in northern Namibia, although less severely affected than in Ovamboland, were nonetheless subjected to similar processes of underdevelopment and subordination to the labour needs of the commercial economy.

7.   Bruwer 1962, pp.7,75-6.
8.   Banghart 1969, p.73; also Moorsom 1977, p.71.
9.   Moorsom 1977, p.64; Bruwer 1962, p.74; Olivier 1961, p.392; Tables 1 and 5.
10. Stellenbosch 1978, Tables 5.7-8.
11. Moorsom 1977, p.68 n.27.

3.2 The Settler Strategy

From the outset, the colonial aim was white settlement. To the South African government the windfall of the German land theft presented a golden opportunity for achieving two primary political objectives: consolidating its hold over Namibia by the settlement of loyal colonists, and finding an outlet for the growing number of landless rural Afrikaners reduced to destitution in South Africa itself by the rapid commercialisation of South African agriculture. In 1920, before the mandate had even been ratified, the South Africans launched a full-scale settlement drive. It was to last 40 years and to be interrupted only by drought and depression in the early 1930s and by the Second World War a decade later. By 1937 the area under commercial farming already included most of the viable stock-raising land on the plateau hardveld. But encroachment did not stop there. Between 1945 and 1959, settlers were pushed into increasingly marginal parts of the sandveld and Namib desert fringe, occupying another 11.1 million hectares. The dry environment required very large ranches; by 1960 a mere 5 000 occupied 40 million hectares — an area larger than that of East and West Germany combined. Table 2 charts the process. The decline in area after 1960 was due to a reorganisation of boundaries by

---

Table 2

The Expansion of Settler Farming[1], 1904-70

	1904	1913	1938	1960	1970/1
No. of farm units[2]	458	1331	3305	5216	4842
Area (million hectares)	4.8	13.4	25.6	39.0	36.0

Notes
1. Excludes Rehoboth Gebiet.
2. Whether 'farms' are units of ownership, management, production or deeds registration is often unclear in the official sources. The Agricultural Census 1959/60 specified 5216 white 'farm owners and renters'; the Odendaal Report gave a total of 6821 surveyed farms (?1962) and the Lands Registry a total of 8803 registered land holdings (1965), both including the Rehoboth Gebiet. More recently, Green has estimated 6500 large-scale 'production units' and 8500 'land holdings'. The figures presented here are intended to indicate units of farm management, which are probably slightly more numerous than the number of proprietors (owning and tenant farmers). Small-scale market gardens, which number anything up to 1000, are presumed to be excluded.

Sources
Wellington 1967, pp.218-9, 312-3, 415; Odendaal Report, p.25; *SWA Handbook* 1967, p.73; *Agricultural Census 1970/1*, Table 1.1; Green 1979, p.22; Green 1981, p.231.

which settlers gained yet more of the hardveld from bantustans, in exchange for larger but less usable areas of sandveld.

From the earliest days white farmers depended heavily upon the state both to gain access to land and to become commercially viable. The Germans gave immigrants extraordinarily comprehensive assistance — subsidies covered settlement, wells, dams, breeding stock, inoculation and losses from disease. This encouraged settlement, but at the price of chronic indebtedness. The South Africans opened up the land to virtually any competent white male applicant, with or without capital. Farms were allocated on leasehold with the option of purchase after five years on 20-year mortgages, and in 1937 fully 40% of farm enterprises were held in this way. The interest rate was subsidised and the purchase price very low, averaging a mere 18 cents per hectare in the 1920s — about 60 cents at 1970 prices — which allowed a settler to pay off the capital cost of an average-sized ranch (8250ha) at only R75 a year plus interest. On top of this, cash loans of up to R1 500 each were available for buying stock and implements and building a house, and the drilling of essential boreholes was done at government expense.

The South African settlement strategy was ultimately successful, although it took a quarter of a century and large-scale state subsidies to achieve. From the early 1940s, commercial agriculture rose from survival to moderate affluence. In the south, ranchers switched rapidly from goats to karakul sheep;[12] in the northern hardveld, stockfarmers progressively abandoned dairy production for beef cattle. Prices, herd sizes and offtake rates all rose, and with them farmers' incomes.[13] By 1965 income per cattle ranch from cattle sales stood at about R8 000, and that of karakul ranches from pelts at R6 500, both assuring the personal wealth of the settler proprietors.

But state support still remained crucial. At times of crisis — prolonged drought, depressed producer prices, epidemic stock disease — state aid was sufficiently generous to guarantee that the great majority of ranchers survived intact, however severe their stock losses. Suspension of loan and interest repayments, minimum product prices or direct price subsidies, and loans or grants for stockfeed, transport, emergency boreholes and grazing, farm wages, even to supplement the farmer's cash income, all provided a comprehensive safety net to

---

12. The karakul is a breed of sheep originating in the steppes of central Asia and is well adapted to a dry environment. Its economic value derives from the pelts of its lambs, which are slaughtered at birth and the pelts manufactured into fur garments for the fashion trade in the affluent West, and to a lesser extent from the meat and wool of the adult animal.

13. 'Offtake rates' here means the number of stock sold annually as a proportion of the total herd at the beginning of the year.

insure the settler farmer against economic disaster.

Increased state emphasis on productivity after 1950 made available further grants and soft loans for a range of improvements, in particular fencing and water supplies. A condition of such aid was that beneficiaries' ranches be comprehensively planned by the Soil Conservation Board, and as many as 90% of settler farms are now so planned. Farm investment climbed steeply in the 1950s and 1960s. The 18 000 boreholes drilled between 1950 and 1960 more than doubled the total number previously sunk. Total indebtedness to the Land Bank nearly quadrupled between 1955 and 1964 to reach over 25% of the total market value of farmland; and in 1968 the bank and other official bodies were the source of 55% of expenditure on farm purchases, at subsidised rates of interest.[14]

State organisation of marketing was also vital. Successful exports were central to the whole colonial enterprise, and agricultural exports were essential if the strategy of settler farming was to be economically viable. For both karakul and cattle ranching, monopoly state marketing boards have been key instruments for market promotion and control. The successful transition in the south to the rearing of karakul sheep, whose pelts are marketed exclusively in the industrial West, was a major fulfilment of this strategy. South Africa also had a direct interest of its own: beef. Until the late 1970s some 80% of Namibian cattle marketed were sent live to South Africa, as well as most chilled, frozen and canned beef. Namibia supplied roughly 20% of South African consumption. It has been used as a variable reserve for covering the gap betwen supply and demand in South Africa — a tap to be turned off whenever (as in the late 1970s) the market was glutted. Except in glut, alternative markets were blocked: in the mid-1950s the authorities even forced the closure of the cold storage plant at Walvis Bay in order to channel all Namibian fresh meat exports to or through South Africa, giving the South African Meat Board a total monopoly over their disposal.[15]

3.3 Farm Labour

The most crucial aspect of state support was the provision of farm labour. It was the point at which the settler strategy interlocked with the creation of reserves — where the robber met the robbed, and put him to work. The viability of settler agriculture was from the start

---

14.   Nixon 1978, pp.1-2; Bähr 1970, p.154; Land and Agricultural Bank of SWA, *Annual Reports*; SWA Administration, *White Paper* 1968, pp.23-4.
15.   Wilken and Fox 1978, pp.53-4.

built upon the exploitation of the labour of black Namibians. This exploitation has partly taken an indirect form through agricultural subsidies funded from tax on profits generated by black workers in other sectors of the economy, and through the hidden subsidies of peasant men and women forced to service the migrant labour system. More directly, it has bound large numbers of black workers to the most poorly paid and repressive conditions of wage-labour of any sector of the commercial economy.

Under settler ranching, the arid environment and sparse vegetation mean that stock must be distributed thinly over the pasture, and herds are regularly moved considerable distances between different areas of grazing, water points and enclosures. On the open range, therefore, efficient pasturing depended on the skill of the herdsmen who accompanied them at all times. By 1956 the number of black farmworkers had risen to about 45 000. The introduction of widespread fencing and camps, however, made possible considerable savings in labour: by 1977, there were probably under 40 000. There was also a major switch, especially on karakul ranches, to casual labour. By 1970/71 over 30% of workers were casual, in employment on average for only about a third of the year. Since the 1930s farmers have also resorted increasingly to contract labour from the north: the standardised migrant contract enabled farmers to undercut even the low wages and bargaining power of their permanent local workers. In 1970/71 contract workers formed about half the regular labour-force, although numbers have declined since. Table 3 shows the overall picture.

For farmworkers, life was frequently a struggle for bare survival. In the words of a government commission in the 1940s, to the karakul shepherd:

is entrusted a flock . . . often worth a couple of thousand pounds . . . Not only has he to bear the responsibility for herding and protecting his flock, but he must do so in wind and rain, in heat and cold, day after day and month after month without a break. For him there is no rest on Sundays or slack periods during the week.

Beatings, fines and witholding of wages were a regular feature of farm work.

Living conditions were no better. In a land where building materials were scarce, few farmers bothered to put up adequate housing and many simply expected their workers to sleep rough in the open or in sheds, with no proper water, cooking, washing and toilet facilities of their own. Access to health care and education was virtually non-existent. Food rations, most of which farmers could not

33

Table 3

The Farm Labour-force[1], 1970/1

	Whites Total	Black workers Men	Black workers Women	Total	Total (Black and White)	Black workers per ranch Cattle[2]	Karakul[2]	All
Regular	517	28 606	1506	30 112	30 629	8.08	3.97	5.88
Casual	60	14 584	930	15 514	15 574	1.63	4.82	3.03
Total	577	43 190	2436	45 626	46 203	9.71	8.79	8.91
House-servants[3]	12	1490	2652	4142	4154	0.84	0.69	0.81
All workers	589	44 680	5088	49 768	50 357	10.55	9.46	9.72

Notes
1. Includes the Rehoboth Gebiet (1 105 black workers).
2. Average of selected districts wholly within the large- and small-stock zones.
3. Figures for house servants probably grossly understated.

Source
Agricultural Census 1970/1, Table 2.1.

34

grow themselves and had to buy in cash, were often so inadequate as to threaten malnutrition, and possibly scurvy where they consisted of maize meal and little else. Few workers could afford to buy adequate clothing and contract workers often had to serve out their 18 months with little more than the regulation issue of shirt, shorts and blanket to survive the cold hardveld winters. Although workers on some farms were permitted to keep a few goats, or occasionally cattle, most ranches were too dry for workers or their families to cultivate garden plots, even if their employers gave them the land or the time to do so.

In such circumstances the buying of essential provisions on credit from the farmer at inflated prices was a chief cause of the chronic indebtedness which held many workers in more or less lifelong debt-bondage. Cash wages were so low as to give workers little chance either of breaking the cycle or of saving. Wages in kind often failed to supply even basic necessities. Workers' own stock, tolerated during the 1920s and 1930s when settlers had spare land and could barely afford to pay cash wages at all, was progressively squeezed out after 1945 by the camp system and rising numbers of stock on the ranches. In 1970/1, when ranch profits were running at an average of some R300-500 per month, the average monthly cash income was a mere R10.25 for regular workers and R6.57 for house-servants, rates which had probably not increased greatly in real terms since the 1920s. For contract workers the maximum possible scale rate was R10.50, the starting minimum a paltry R3.75.

Such extreme exploitation, made economically possible by the reserve and migrant labour system, was reinforced by a battery of legislation dating back to German times. A vagrancy law made any black without a labour contract liable to be arrested and forcibly contracted to a local employer. According to a South African representative in the 1920s, 'farmers . . . were frequently to be seen standing outside the magistrate's court waiting for persons up for judgement to be convicted in order to hire them'. Once bound to a white employer, there was little chance of escape by legal means. The pass law (Proclamation 11-22) made all blacks unable to show an employer's pass to the police on demand when outside their place of work or residence liable to immediate arrest, punishment and return to the employer, even if they were attempting to register a complaint against their employer with the police.

In addition, a draconian masters and servants law (Proclamation 34-20) made 'desertion' a serious office and gave their 'masters' sweeping disciplinary powers. While permanent farmworkers, who were commonly able to insist on nominal monthly contracts, retained a limited right to change jobs and seek better wages and conditions, the contracts (in reality indentures) of northern migrant workers prevented them from even attempting to negotiate their wage-rates or give notice. The unpopularity of farm contracts meant that most were inexperienced first-time recruits still in their teens. Indeed, the SWANLA grading system, under which all those deemed unfit for ordinary labouring jobs in the mines and towns were classified 'C' and sent to domestic service or farms, was a thinly-disguised device for channelling child labour to the ranches, a sizeable proportion of 'C' grade herders being adolescents under the legal minimum age of 15.

Despite the severity of colonial oppression, black farmworkers have been far from passive victims of the dehumanising conditions they have been forced to ensure. Active and underground resistance has been persistent throughout the colonial period. The traumatic experience of the genocide and land theft continues as a living historical tradition amongst descendants of the survivors. Contract workers developed a strong tradition of informal solidarity, and as early as the 1940s farmers were complaining of organised 'desertions' from groups of neighbouring farms, and that the ill-treatment they called 'discipline' caused their workers to vanish without trace. The workers' awareness of the contribution of their labour to the conspicuous prosperity of their employers was to be expressed dramatically in the great national strike of 1971-2. Popular expectations at independence will be moulded by the fact that some of those now working on settler farms are living on land their 19th century ancestors occupied before the German conquest; that many reserve residents may wish to reclaim ancestoral land; and that many farmworkers, whatever their pre-colonial origins, see themselves as having a right to the soil their labour has made productive.

4 Agriculture Today: Structure and Crisis

4.1 The Structure of Settler Farming

Agriculture today is in deep crisis under the triple impact of drought, war and structural change. The longer-term structural problems are perhaps most crucial for the future. In this respect, the settler farming sector imposed on Namibia in this century is fundamentally flawed. There are six structural weaknesses which indicate how distorted the colonial economy has become.

First, production is almost entirely for export, regardless of Namibian needs, and is concentrated on two main products. Cattle, dairy produce and hides realise about 55% of total sales, karakul ranching another 35-40%. All karakul pelts and 92% of cattle are exported. Other forms of commercial agriculture are either secondary aspects of stock-raising or very limited in scope. Dairy farming has declined: the marketed output of butter and cheese realised almost as much as cattle in 1936, but by 1974/75 had declined to only 6% of its peak level, reached in the early 1950s.[1] Only for perhaps 500 farms in the Otavi highlands are cereals, fruit and vegetables, which have a local market, an important part of gross output.

Secondly, the ranches are highly capitalised. Methods of production are severely constrained by the arid or semi-arid climate. The low carrying capacity of the land and the large size of individual herds and flocks — about 800 head per cattle ranch and 1 250 head per karakul ranch in 1977 — has created extensive units of pasture management (Table 4). An increasing proportion of ranchers have enclosed their land into fenced camps, which, as animals are moved from one camp to another, allow them to be spread more evenly over the grazing area, and enable sections of the ranch to be held in reserve

---

1. Bähr 1968, Table 20; *Windhoek Advertiser* 27 Oct. 1975.

Table 4

Settler Ranching: Land and Stock, c.1970

Land Use Zone	area (million hectares)	farms (no.)	average area per farm (ha)	average herd size per farm cattle	average herd size per farm karakul
Mixed farming	2.75	540	5090	500	65
Stock-raising: large	8.6	1300	6615	580	340
transitional	7.8	1083	7200	490	830
small	16.85	1920	8780	100	1520
Total	*36.0*	*4843*	*7435*	*357*	*889*

Notes
Rehoboth Gebiet excluded. All figures approximate.

Sources
Agricultural Census 1961/2 (Odendaal Report, p.273) and 1970/71; maps and land-use data.

---

for the inevitable droughts. On karakul ranches this has been combined in many cases with boundary fencing proof against the most dangerous predator of small stock, the jackal. Such fencing not only decreases stock losses but also dispenses with round-the-clock guarding of the flocks, thereby permitting more efficient night grazing. Here too the camp system facilitates periodic supplementary feeding, which improves stock condition generally and in particular assists farmers to bring more ewes up from two to three lambings every two years. By 1969/70 the average in the heart of the cattle zone was 16 camps of 377ha each per farm, and a survey in the mid-1970s reported a national average of 22 camps per farm at roughly 350ha each, indicating that the enclosure of the land was far advanced.[2]

Two other principal methods of improving productivity have been employed. First, the crossing of indigenous with foreign strains has produced cattle and karakul cross-breeds which are well adapted to the fierceness of the dry, sub-tropical environment. Second, supplementary stockfeeds, both imported and home grown, have been widely used to cover pasture deficiencies and periods of drought, and to a certain extent as a general means of increasing the number of beasts on the land. As a result, the levels of output and productivity are high. Karakul exports in 1974-80 averaged 2.8m. pelts, or about 1.15 lambs for every ewe on the white ranches. Cattle ranches sell about 20% of the herd each year, compared with only 10% on

---

2. Carstens 1971, Table 7; Wilcox 1976, p.27, citing undated survey.

communal land in Botswana. So neither the gross volume nor the rate of production is likely to be capable of substantial long-term increase by further investments on the pattern pursued since the Second World War.

However, and this is the third structural weakness, it must be doubted whether settler stockfarming as a whole is economically viable by its own commercial standards. Although statistics on farm income and costs are sketchy, it appears that the rate of return on the current value of invested capital (including land) has generally been well below prevailing interest and inflation rates (see Tables A7 and A8). The figure of 6.24% from a 1969/70 survey of northern cattle ranches compares with estimates of 4-5% for better than average cattle ranches on the central hardveld and karakul ranches around Maltahöhe in the early 1970s, and as little as 2% nationally at the 1970/1 agricultural census. Furthermore, official estimates reported by Nixon in 1978 point to a great disparity in profitability between ranches, the return being 8.1% for those in the top 20% net income bracket — still very low — but a mere 2.2% for those in the 50-60 percentile. Indeed, if the rancher's personal income is deducted from the net profit at the prevailing rate for middle managers or civil servants, the average return on ranch capital becomes nil or even negative in most years. Botswana studies confirm that large-scale investment in ranching yields low returns. Such a conclusion may seem paradoxical in view of the physical efficiency of ranches — but the point is that this efficiency has been achieved only by sinking an enormous quantity of capital. Capital investment is much larger — and also freer of debt, because of government subsidy — than it would have been had farmers been forced to compete with more profitable sectors of the economy for funds. It is the logical result of an agricultural policy intent on maximising the volume of production at all costs, first by bringing even highly marginal land into production, then by increasing productivity through capital-intensive methods.

That policy, in turn, stems from the colonial pre-occupation with getting the maximum number of South African settlers on to the land. Because the size of new ranches was generally set near the minimum judged necessary to support a single resident owner and family, incoming settlers had to maximise their output simply to achieve the high standard of living which they expected as whites. State assistance consistently favoured individual owner-occupiers rather than partnerships or companies owning several ranches. The result is another apparent paradox, and the fourth structural feature: despite all the investment, income per ranch averaged no more than the middle range of white salaries in the towns and mines, and on the poorer ranches a good deal less. South African settlement strategy has in effect created an inflated colony of over-capitalised ranchers whose high levels of personal consumption absorb a disproportionate share of the income which their expensively efficient output generates.

Fifthly, there is an ecological cost. Little is known about the depletion of groundwater, but wide areas are now subject to controls on the spacing of boreholes and the rate of pumping. Pasture degeneration is more obvious. In some places the Namib desert encroached 50km or more before the administration 'solved' the problem by buying out its settlers and transferring the area to the Damaraland bantustan. On the northern hardveld, Wellington noted as long ago as the mid-1960s that 'owing to faulty farming practices perennial species have been replaced in many parts of the area by inferior annual grasses and there is a continuous encroachment by thorn scrub'. In the dry north-western district of Outjo it was estimated in 1981 that 31% of the total surface area, and an even higher proportion of the grazing, had been engulfed by permanent bush encroachment, a devastating indictment of little more than half a century of settler ranching in the area.[3]

At the heart of what is potentially a serious ecological crisis lies once again the policy of maximising settler farming. One of the most fundamental contradictions in a semi-arid environment is the ecological rigidity of relatively small-scale private enterprise farming in an environment which requires flexible methods and very extensive units of pasture management. The division of the hardveld into a mosaic of fixed separate ranches deprived stockfarming of the mobility over wide areas which in pre-colonial times was a crucial means of coping with an unreliable rainfall.

On marginal ranches especially, the drive to maximise output has been a powerful incentive to overstock. Since droughts mask long-term degeneration in the vegetation, many settlers adopt a short-term perspective, increasing stock numbers rapidly before the pasture has had time to recover from drought, overstocking during good years, and retaining too many animals when drought sets in once more. Even the camp system, which can double the potential yield of natural grazing, can damage the pasture if too many cattle are brought on. A study of the sandveld north of Gobabis found precisely this condition on marginal ranches, which had taken advantage of cheap state credit to invest in camps. During the 1950s and 1960s overgrazing had led to grass regression and bush encroachment, progressively turning the pasture into browse more suitable for sheep and goats than cattle. A trickle of sub-marginal ranchers have been abandoning the land for

---

3.   Wellington 1967, p.60; *Windhoek Advertiser* 21 Aug. 1981.

good. It is unlikely that this area is an isolated example,[4]

Sixthly, the viability of ranching depends on access to particular, limited markets, controlled by highly centralised marketing organisations. Meat exports, except for canned beef, are controlled entirely by the Meat Board. Although an increasing proportion is now slaughtered locally, nearly all chilled and frozen meat, as well as live exports, goes direct to South Africa. Karakul pelts, on the other hand, are destined mostly for Europe, 80% for Germany and Italy, where they are used in luxury fashions. Namibia accounts for about a quarter of the total number of pelts sold in the West, and so relies on the whim of fashion designers continuing to turn to karakul. For this advertising is crucial and the South African and Namibian state karakul boards, using the joint trade name SWAKARA, have spent heavily since the 1950s on promotions in Europe and North America, and more recently also in Japan.

The actual marketing of karakul pelts is in the hands of two international fur companies, Hudson's Bay and Annings (Canada/UK) and Eastwood and Holt (UK/SA), which dispose of over 90% of Namibian karakul exports at the regular trade auctions, held mainly in London. Both firms are supplied by large South African-controlled farmer cooperatives, whose Namibian interests have recently (1981) been merged in a single government-sponsored cooperative, Agra, which collects directly from the ranches or from district collecting points. Nearly all the initial sorting is done at Hudson's Bay's large sorting centre in Windhoek, which was opened in 1969. Each pelt is coded with the producer's identity number and the entire operation is computerised. Such narrow and unreliable export markets, and so high a degree of South African and foreign company control, constitute a serious threat to economic viability and future Namibian control: a threat demonstrated by the recent collapse in the markets for both beef and karakul.

These six weaknesses together mean great difficulties for any incoming government: the sector is doubtful both economically and ecologically, demands a high state and skilled manpower input, and does not meet Namibia's own food needs. But the position has deteriorated dramatically since 1977.

4.2 The Present Crisis in Settler Farming

The careful colonial creation of a patchwork of settler ranches is today disintegrating. Economic weaknesses have been exposed by

---

4.   Leser 1975.

drought. Pressed by the liberation movement, South African colonial strategists have abandoned their settler dream. Agriculture is in deep crisis.

The settler ideal has already been eroded. Rising land prices in the 1960s blocked new entrants. Wealthier farm-owners have moved to the towns, visiting only at intervals and leaving the day-to-day management in the hands of white or black supervisors: one recent source, relying on official information, estimated in 1976 that as many as 48% of all Namibian farm enterprises had absentee owners.[5] Furthermore in marginal areas ownership has become more concentrated, as the unsuccessful leave and others expand their holdings to create more viable economic units. Representative data are almost non-existent, but a study in the mid-1960s of part of the eastern cattle-raising district of Gobabis found that 16% of the farmers owned two-fifths of the farmed area.[6] South African and West German company investment in the ranching sector has also expanded, and at least one Walvis Bay fishing company was buying up land during the 1970s.

In the late 1970s the Namibian climate entered one of its periodic cycles of prolonged and severe drought. By mid-summer 1982 parts of the north were entering the sixth year and the south the fifth year of a drought at least as devastating as its three major 20th-century predecessors.

The stocking of the ranching zone to capacity and beyond during the preceding years of normal rainfall was bound to lead to severe mortality amongst stock. The settlers used their wealth and credit to move stock to less affected areas (especially in South Africa) as well as to buy stockfeed and drill boreholes. In April 1981 the government announced a comprehensive programme in support: the funds averaged some R10 000 per settler ranch, in addition to subsidies for wages and karakul sales. However, such short-term measures could not prevail — and in practice it is unclear how much of the promised aid materialised. By January 1982 it was officially estimated that the national cattle herd had shrunk by two-thirds, from 2.5m to 0.85m, and karakul sheep were being slaughtered on a large scale.[7] Settlers — as opposed to black farmers — were able to preserve much of their wealth, but only by selling their herds rather than watch them die; in the Namibia of today, many may leave rather than reinvest. Settler stock-farming appears to be in dire straits.

Its plight has been compounded by serious marketing difficulties.

5.   Wilcox 1976, p.26.
6.   Stengel 1966, p.41.
7.   *Windhoek Advertiser* 7 Jan. 1982.

The government imposed severe quota restrictions on sales to South Africa, which delayed the off-loading of surplus cattle and led to widespread corruption in which smaller farmers lost out. Furthermore a 37% fall in real terms in slaughter stock prices between 1974/5 and 1978/9 made the returns on those cattle that could be marketed increasingly uneconomic. By the time prices began to climb again and quotas were lifted (1979-81), cattle ranches were deep into the drought.

Meanwhile the auction prices for karakul pelts became increasingly volatile (1975-9), and then suddenly collapsed, averaging in 1981 little more than half the level of the previous year. The number of pelts marketed dropped by 37% during 1981 and in early 1982 was running some 60% below the level two years previously as ranchers sold off their flocks to the abattoirs.[8] This seems to reflect a permanent shift in Western fashion away from karakul fur — now regarded in the crucial West German market as out of date. In the United States, as a recent report to the Windhoek-based International Karakul Secretariat poignantly put it: 'In the East, Persian lamb is remembered, and many of the old coats were handed down to black house servants. So not only does the grandmother stigma remain, but an association with black nannies.'[9]

Drought was the immediate cause of collapse, but the system had been undermined during the 1970s by a sustained challenge from black workers and the Namibian liberation movement SWAPO. The 1971/72 contract workers' strike, although concentrated in the mines and towns, drew in workers from the countryside as well, as news spread by word of mouth and on news bulletins. That these despised units of labour-power could act with such impressive and powerful unity came as a severe shock to the self-confidence of the white ranchers. The strike, and the worker militancy which followed, produced the first major crack in the framework of labour repression, and began the erosion of the privileged position of farmers in the national labour market. New recruiting arrangements meant that farmers now had to compete with better-paying sectors. At the same time, contract workers increasingly undermined the system, many deserting , simply using the farm contract as a stepping-stone to town. By 1976 the number of contract workers in farm employment had dropped by more than 10 000 in five years to only 6 000.

More recently the growing power of the liberation movement has brought large sections of the white farming community into the front line of the conflict between South Africa's army of occupation and the

---

8. *Windhoek Advertiser* 28 Aug. 1981, 10 Dec. 1981, 8 Jan. 1981.
9. Battelle 1981, p.146.

guerrilla units of the People's Liberation Army of Namibia (PLAN), SWAPO's military wing. Since 1976 PLAN cadres have operated continuously, sometimes in considerable strength, in the heart of the white cattle-ranching zone (Tsumeb — Grootfontein — Otjiwarongo districts). On 10 May 1979 the South Africa authorities extended martial law to the whole of the white farming region north of Windhoek and began a substantial military build-up in the north of the area. The Chief of Staff SWA Command nevertheless admitted in February 1980 that the South African Defence Force (SADF) was unable to guarantee farmers safety of transport or even of their premises.[10]

The new state strategy

More seriously, the advance of the liberation movement has forced South Africa to adopt a new colonial strategy which no longer revolves around settlers. The Turnhalle arrangements created a central government apparatus over which the all-white Legislative Assembly, still dominated by the farming interest, now has little control. In order to win internal and international credibility South Africa has eased its racial restrictions on movement, social segregation and property ownership, and removed farmers' legal hold over their workers — at each stage overriding the rearguard opposition of organised white agriculture. Economically, the hugely profitable corporate mining sector is the engine which fuels the remodelled bantustan programme; politically, the backbone of the occupation regime is no longer the rural settler community but the full-time and reservist formations of the SADF.

Indeed South Africa's main interest in settlers is now military. The widening of the war zone has made white farmers in the north a crucial second line of defence for the occupation regime — with the fortification of farmhouses subsidised — and has placed a premium on keeping them on the land. Alarmed at the scale of rural depopulation, the South Africans have pumped in large amounts of state funds. During the first half of 1980 the Windhoek administration launched two subsidised land settlement schemes, both to dissuade existing farmers from leaving and to resettle abandoned ranches. One of them was applied specifically to the northern edge of the farm zone — 888 farms in all. It lowered interest rates on state credit below even the existing subsidised levels, made such loans available for 100% mortgages on land purchase, for virtually any capital expenditure and up to 50% of debt liabilities, and paid out an annual R2 000 in cash to each farmer who simply resided on his land throughout the year. The

---

10.   *Windhoek Observer* 1 Mar. 1980.

South Africans' overriding preoccupation with counter-insurgency is exposed in the strings attached to the package: that applicants be 'an approved asset in regard to security', join the local commando, live continuously on their farms, and be barred from selling without government permission for ten years.

These measures have clearly not stemmed the tide. In 1980 the number of cattle ranchers registered with the Meat Board fell by 12%. Essential breeding stock is being sold (females were 48% of sales in mid-1979, compared with 38% in 1976).[11] On the fringes of the cattle zone the flight from the land has approached crisis proportions. Already by early 1976 the selling price of farms in Outjo, Tsumeb and Grootfontein districts had collapsed to a fraction of their previous levels; in some cases auctioneers had difficulty finding buyers at any price. By May 1978 as many as 40% of settlers in Grootfontein district had left their farms; by August 1981 only 49% of farms in Outjo district were still occupied by old-established settlers and another 5% were up for sale. Although here, as around Gobabis, there has been a spate of land purchases at inflated prices by bantustans, over a third of the farms remain empty, and it is resident white farmers rather than absentee owners who are selling up.[12] The long-term commitment of many white farmers to their enterprises must now be in serious doubt.

4.3 The Structure of Peasant Farming

No less than settler farming, peasant agriculture has been continually undermined by drought and war, while the underlying structure of overcrowding and dependence on migrant labour remains largely unaltered. This section examines the state of peasant agriculture in the mid to late 1970s and then looks at the consequences of government policy and natural disaster.

Neither the bantustan boundaries nor the earlier division of the country into the 'Police Zone' and the 'Northern Zone' provides anything like an adequate framework for the analysis of peasant agriculture, and it would be doing a disservice to the consideration of post-liberation development priorities to perpetuate their use except where required by the context or by the organisation of official statistics.[13] In practice the areas of peasant occupation, as we have

11. *Kontak* Aug. 1980, p.2 Table 2.
12. *Windhoek Advertiser* 23 Jan. 1976, 22 & 24 March 1977, 23 & 24 May 1978, 22 May 1981, 29 Aug. 1981, *Cape Times* 25 & 27 May 1981.
13. For similar reasons the names of the bantustans, which reflect the ethnic categories of apartheid and the artificial tribal 'homelands' it sets out to create, have been given in quotation marks.

seen, fall into four of the basic zones of ecology and land-use (see Maps 3 and 5). They include small and poor areas of the three stock-raising zones, and a larger proportion of the mixed farming zone in the far north, where a greater abundance of rainfall and surface water permits both pastoral and arable agriculture.

In the dry sandveld areas of all these zones scattered groups of hunter-gatherers continue to survive in the spaces between peasant and ranch settlement, but cattle-raising and nature reserves have encroached far into the land. Attention here is therefore confined to stock farmers and mixed farming, the predominant forms of land use in the areas where an adequate water supply is available.

(a) Stock-farmers

In the reserves on and around the edges of the interior hardveld, stock-raising is the principal form of agriculture, with the proportion of cattle to small-stock rising from south to north. It is today a cash as well as a subsistence economy, depending on sales of stock and even more on income from migrant labour. Arable farming is limited to garden plots and the occasional dryland maize or wheat field-crop, mostly in sandy stream beds in the less arid northwest of 'Hereroland' and the east of 'Damaraland' and around the few strong springs in the Kaokoveld. Any assessment of agriculture in these areas is bedevilled by an almost complete lack of reliable and up-to-date data. The inherent agricultural limitations are nevertheless painfully self-evident. Since most of the reserves were deliberately located on inferior farming land, black stock-farmers are confronted with serious environmental constraints.

The lack of reliable water supplies is the most formidable of these constraints. Surface waterholes or wells are generally scarce and yields are low and unreliable. Nor are boreholes or dams more promising. In the south the underlying rock formations of the Fish River valley, which the 'Namaland' bantustan straddles, generally yield only small quantities of notoriously brackish groundwater, and there is little scope for trapping surface run-off in dams. In the 'Damaraland' bantustan groundwater appears to be limited and unevenly distributed. Over much of the eastern sandveld ('Hereroland'), groundwater is very deep and difficult to extract. In addition, in the south ('Namaland') and northwest ('Kaokoland') the rugged terrain reduces the soil cover and the extent of the pasturage. In the sandveld serious mineral and especially protein deficiencies in the grazing pose problems for stock-raising even where water is to be had.

The colonial regime imposed overcrowded bantustans on these areas in the interests of migrant labour. The result is extreme cycles: animal numbers build up in good years to levels which damage the

46

pasture, but then fall dramatically in a prolonged drought. Official statistics, for what they are worth, suggest that between the end of the last major drought cycle and the beginning of the present one (1962 and 1978-9 respectively), the number of 'livestock units' doubled in 'Namaland' and 'Hereroland' and more than quadrupled in 'Damaraland' and the Rehoboth Gebiet. In 'Namaland', even at the optimistic official estimate of carrying capacity, there was in 1979 a 15% excess of stock overall.[14] In 'Damaraland' and 'Hereroland' skilled pastoralists had managed to build up high stock levels on land so marginal as to have been virtually excluded from the stock-farming zone of their pre-colonial ancestors. But, as the next section shows, the recent drought has decimated these herds.

The bantustans in the large-stock zone seem better placed than elsewhere: very rough calculations of income from sales there in 1979 suggest an average income from the sale of cattle of around R1 000 per household from roughly 7 head of cattle each. In contrast, in the southern reserves income from sales of stock and karakul pelts yielded only R200 per household; and in Ovamboland income from cattle, virtually the only marketable commodity, averaged at most R30 per household and probably less (see Appendix, Table A6).

However, these averages conceal considerable variations. In the large-stock reserves, a handful of farmers, frequently in collaboration with the bantustan authorities, have managed to beat the colonial restrictions and accumulate considerable wealth and influence. Often they combine cattle farming with other income from trade or transport contracting or posts in administration or education. Until recently, however, colonial discrimination prevented them from becoming fully-fledged commercial ranchers, able to buy ranches away from the crowded reserves, and their herds have suffered substantial losses in the recent drought. These large herds raise the figure for average cash income in the large-stock bantustans; the majority of cattle owners earn considerably less. The general picture countrywide is that bantustan land is too poor in pasture and water, and overcrowding too severe, for peasant stock-farming to be anything but a pale imitation of its 19th century form; most households depend on income from migrant labour.

(b) Arable farmers
The cultivated areas of the northern sandveld contain fully half of the black population of Namibia on a mere 3.2% of the land surface, or about 6% if the adjacent seasonal pasture is included. The remains of

---

14.   Odendaal 1964, Table C; *Kontak* April 1980, p.3, Tables 2-3; SA, Dept. of Coloured Relations, *Annual Report* 1979, 1980.

pre-colonial agriculture are deeply undermined, and households look elsewhere for most of their income — we have already seen that in 1974 only a third came from the land. Agriculture nevertheless remains important.

Higher rainfall permits a far greater intensity of land use than elsewhere in Namibia. The key in the centre of the region is the flat Ovambo floodplain. Here low average rainfall and drought make grain cultivation precarious, and endemic disease and scarce pasture create a constant risk of poor condition and high mortality amongst stock. Closer settlement of the land, though risky, is nevertheless viable. Farming here is diversified. Stock-farming is one of the pillars of the peasant economy. Roughly a quarter of the national herds of cattle and goats, and a third of poultry, are owned by farmers in the north. Cattle are predominant, almost exclusively so in the Okavango valley and the eastern Caprivi Strip, but to a lesser extent in Ovamboland, where goats are nearly as numerous.

In arable farming the staple grain is pearl millet (*mahangu*), which is well adapted to dry conditions. According to official estimates, whose reliability is uncertain, millet yields 35 000-40 000 tonnes in years of good rainfall, most of it in Ovamboland (Table 5). Sorghum adds about another 5 000 tonnes in Ovamboland — only in exceptional years can it reach 20 000 tonnes. Towards the east, as the level and reliability of rainfall improves, maize increases in importance, becoming the main crop in the eastern Caprivi Strip. Overall, a total grain harvest of around 50 000 tonnes is probable in the peasant areas of the mixed farming zone in years of average rainfall, with much less in time of drought. As in pre-colonial times, vegetables become invaluable sources of food or moisture when the cereals fail. Fresh-water fish are extensively caught.

As well as being diversified, peasant farming in the north is also integrated. Nearly all peasant households are engaged in each of the major branches of production and few specialise in particular

---

Table 5

Official Estimates of Peasant Millet Production in the North, 1970-78

(tonnes)	1970	1975	1976	1977	1978
	32 700	35 800	41 600	40 300	25 000

Source
Namibia/SWA Prospectus 1980, Table 6.

48

products to the exclusion of others. In Ovamboland in particular this has created a complex seasonal cycle of production requiring considerable managerial skill to organise. The planting and harvesting sequence for the vegetable crops must be carefully coordinated with the main grain crops, which, if labour permits, may have to be replanted if the early rains fall. Livestock must be kept away from the fields during the growing period and found pasture in conditions of permanent scarcity. However carefully the production cycle is arranged, there are inevitably peaks in the demand for labour-time, chiefly in the sowing period of early summer and the harvesting time of autumn. Today, migrant labour and the war make it hard to meet these peaks.

In the Okavango valley the shape of agriculture is similar but less precarious: the soil is slightly more fertile, the rainfall a little higher and more regular, the sandveld pasture more accessible, and river fish and drinking water readily available throughout the year. Field cultivation, chiefly of millet, is located on the terraces along the sides of the narrow valley (up to 10km wide); while cattle are pastured alternately along the wet season streams (*omuramba*) of the sandveld to the south and by the banks of the river itself once the seasonal floodwaters have receded. In the eastern Caprivi Strip, the river margins are generally too swampy for permanent settlement. Here the people are grouped into small villages on drier ground and the higher rainfall allows more maize and a greater variety of tropical fruit to be grown.

Within its limits, peasant agriculture in the north is both resourceful and efficient, particularly in grain cultivation. Everywhere the soil is little better than pure sand. It is severely deficient in mineral and organic nutrients and becomes rapidly waterlogged during the rainy season, particularly in the *oshana* zone. Here, however, the specialised techniques developed over the centuries by Ovambo peasants have built up a shallow but moderately fertile topsoil from which the salts have been leached down to lower levels. The grain yield has been estimated at a low 2.5 bags per hectare, but may well be higher.

Nevertheless, this yield is won at a high price in physical effort. Fields must be laboriously cleared, sown, weeded and harvested by hand, and at any stage a prolonged dry spell, abnormal floods or insect pests may ruin months of hard labour. In the Okavango valley soils are reasonable and ploughs became widespread in the 1940s. In Ovamboland, however, ploughs are even now not universal, and hoes still in use. In part this reflects the poor soils: deep tractor-drawn ploughing risks damaging the fragile soil structure and bringing up the saline sub-soil. Even the more-widely practised light ploughing with donkeys may leave problems of drainage. Ploughing is also more risky than hoeing: because the whole crop is planted at one time, it can be destroyed by a dry period, whereas a hoed crop is planted over a number of weeks and only part would suffer from the same brief drought. Hoeing can also start earlier, before the rain comes. But hoeing is back-breaking work. When cash incomes rose after the increases in migrant workers' wages in the 1970s, people increasingly switched from hoes to ploughs. The long-term effect of this change on soils needs early research after independence.

The picture therefore is of an efficient but low-technology agriculture, severely strained by the absence of men and by over-crowding. In the stock-raising reserves a handful of large cattle-owners have prospered, but the vast majority are deeply dependent on wage remittances or the miserably low state pensions. In the northern mixed farming reserves, denied effective markets for their produce, food output in all but exceptional years is well below the needs of the resident population, let alone the tens of thousands of migrant workers forced out by poverty. Colonial policy bears the responsibility.

4.4 South African Policy in the Bantustans

For fifty years, colonial policy was to neglect and isolate the reserves in order to preserve rural homes for the families of migrant labourers. The key was that most households retain access to land, and to that end, the administration sought to prevent wide differences in wealth emerging in the reserves. Not for Namibia the provision of credit or 'model farmer' schemes of other colonial regimes, which might sharpen the distinction between poor and cash-cropping peasants; nor enclosure of the land (so creating a landless class) which South Africa promoted in the more desperately overcrowded parts of its own bantustans. Black stock-farmers were excluded from the extensive state support provided to the white ranchers, and were deprived of direct access to markets; almost the only way of selling was through official auctions, and even these were not widely held in the northern reserves before the 1970s. In the stock-farming reserves, cattle herds about 100 head and small stock herds above 300 were simply forbidden — the average on white ranches being about 800 and 1 250 respectively. The lynchpin of the system was communal land tenure — which compelled wealthy stock-farmers to compete on the open range for scarce pasture and water. It was also the chief mechanism by which the tribal hierarchy, and so the colonial regime, controlled all major aspects of peasant life.

These policies have increasingly failed in their aim of creating an artificial equality of poverty. The growing land shortage has left a minority of rural households with little or no access to land or livestock of their own. Another small group, especially those collaborating with the bantustan administrations, has been able to accumulate wealth and economic influence. The deepening dependence of most peasant households on wage remittances has stimulated the growth of rural traders and transport contractors, many of them small-scale, but a few wealthy and economically powerful amongst an impoverished people. On the whole, colonial policy has restrained these tendencies; but the lines of social division are nonetheless being gradually more sharply drawn.

The 1964 Odendaal Report marked a fundamental change in South African political strategy. It attempted to head off the growing challenge of the nationalist movement — SWAPO had been founded in 1960 — by introducing fully fledged bantustans complete with client tribal 'governments'. For each of the ten 'nations' it claimed to have identified, the colonial regime set about consolidating a bantustan out of the existing reserves.

In agriculture, however, little changed as a result of Odendaal. Communal land tenure, and the objectives behind it, remained intact. Although some land has been transferred, popular resistance still prevents the South Africans completing the removal of 'black spots' on the hardveld, and they themselves seem to have balked at disentangling the populations of the reserves so as to create pure ethnic 'homelands'. State services underwent a limited improvement. High quality veterinary services were extended, especially in the southern reserves — good services protect the nearby settler herds. In the north, dipping facilities have been widely installed, the incidence of tsetse-fly in the Caprivi Strip reduced, and general inoculation introduced, but there are few signs yet of significant impact on the numerous endemic diseases and parasites. Three research stations were set up in the reserves in the 1960s and training facilities were added in the 1970s, including agricultural schools in Ovamboland and on the Okavango River.

Virtually the only capital works to benefit the peasantry directly has been water infrastructure in the Ovambo floodplain. Elsewhere the development of water resources in the reserves was slow and unsystematic, but in Ovamboland from the mid 1950s onwards a network of small dams was built, drawing their supply from the *oshana*. The regional distribution of the summer floodwaters was evened out during the 1960s by two canals running south-east along the courses of the two largest *oshana* in the western half of the floodplain. In 1973 these canals began to receive water pumped from the Calueque dam situated on the Kunene River across the Angolan border. These measures have increased, but more importantly stabilised, the water supply during the dry season and droughts. They have probably been a major factor in the continued growth of the stock population.

Overall, South Africa has devoted substantial resources in recent years to the development of water supplies in Namibia, but this has had less to do with the needs of agriculture than with the escalating demand of Namibia's towns and large mines for both water and power. The Department of Water Affairs has taken the lead in formulating a comprehensive long-term national development plan and securing a high level of capital funding. At its heart was the Kunene hydro-electric scheme, which was designed to double the installed electrical capacity of Namibia; it was only as a by-product that half the projected water supply could be allocated to Ovamboland. Similarly, the major pilot irrigation scheme at Hardap Dam near Mariental is in white ranchland — and the major soil surveys for full-scale irrigation using Kunene water have been in the settler cattle area rather than Ovamboland.

It seems that, even within Ovamboland, agriculture is not the highest priority for water supply and the potential of the system is not fully realised. Data are scanty, but it appears that the primary use of the western canal and pipeline system is to fill the dams serving the principal settlements, including army camps. Cattle can drink from the old canal south of Ogongo, and from watering points along the pipeline to Oshivelo. However, the canal does not always have water in it, and the planned network of feeder pipelines stretching eastwards has not been built. The liberation of Angola also forced the installation of a substitute pumping station at the Ruacana Falls, which could deliver only a tenth of the planned supply.

Behind South Africa's mostly low-key and limited initiatives lies a contradictory attitude towards the Namibian peasantry. The official model for agrarian development is the high output, profit-making entrepreneur. Research in the north, for example, has concentrated on large-scale intensive methods on enclosed land. But this is remote from the actual needs of peasant farmers on overcrowded land, and also contradicts the whole theory behind South Africa's belief in communal land tenure. In practice, the bulk of state investment in the bantustans has gone into physical infrastructure rather than support for small farmers — or indeed not into agriculture at all. The parastatal First National Development Corporation (FNDC) has concentrated attention on the promotion of black traders, rather than farmers, and on a number of factories. Of the latter, the Eloolo meat cannery at Oshakati is the only one to serve peasant farmers directly, though it also maintains its own herd of some 40 000 cattle.

The DTA's view of the future

With the advent of South Africa's 'internal settlement' for Namibia, the principles behind the migrant labour reserves have been called into question for the first time. On the one hand, the interest of the dominant mining companies in migrant labour is no longer so strong. On the other, the DTA, having nailed its colours to the mast of unrestrained capitalist growth, has become acutely aware of the numerical insignificance of the black business class. In admitting that few black Namibians had any stake in 'free enterprise', DTA leader Dirk Mudge concluded his 1980 budget speech by declaring that 'we shall have to help such people to also share in the benefits of private land ownership, be this in the farming areas or in the urban area; and by so doing, give them something to live for, or if necessary to die for'.[15]

To a large extent, this is being attempted by opening the settler ranching area to the very few prosperous and politically 'sound' blacks. A 1980 scheme allowed the state to buy farms on behalf of prospective full time settlers who would then lease then on heavily subsidised terms with the option of purchase after 15 years. Land Bank loans were made available to favoured individuals, although official embarrassment at abuses has led them to be curbed. Straight purchases by bantustan authorities of dozens of settler ranches in 1980 and 1981 — ostensibly for emergency grazing — may also have the same effect, at least for some bantustans such as 'Hereroland'.

The law has also been amended to allow bantustan administrations to enclose and divide communal land for settlement schemes. In 1978 the Department of Coloured Affairs began to demarcate and fence off 'economic farming units' in 'Namaland', which it administered. By mid-1980 51 such units had been identified, although only seven were completed and none as yet occupied. At the same time, subsidies for 'farm development and soil conservation' were made available on the same terms as for white and Rehoboth farmers. A loan scheme for livestock was introduced, under which R161 000 had been lent by mid-1980.[16] As yet, however, there has been no general move to extend enclosure and agricultural credit along these lines to the large-stock and arable zones further north, where the vested political and economic interest in communal tenure is strongest. Were it to happen, the consequences for those made landless would be devastating.

---

15. *On the Economic Front*, 2, June 1980.
16. SA, Dept. of Coloured Relations, *Annual Report* 1979, p.13; 1980, pp.9-10.

The major project for boosting small-scale farming in the north certainly presupposes individual rather than communal control of land. In 1980 a FNDC spokesman stated that its strategy was to set up 'satellites' around profitable 'energy centres'. Emphasis would be on community development and more specifically on identifying, training and assisting approved individual farmers. The centre could provide services to the satellites, such as financial assistance, training, expertise and certain raw materials, and would also act as a marketing channel for their products.[17] In 1981 this was supposedly under way using one of FNDC's four Okavango Valley irrigation schemes as the 'energy centre' for irrigated crops, and treating its Mangetti cattle ranch similarly.

Yet these FNDC schemes expose a second contradiction in official policy, intrinsic to the repressive nature of the regime: its policies reflect the authoritarian methods by which it holds power. The main agricultural effort in the north has gone into five irrigated estates (Table 6), and the large cattle ranch at Mangetti. For all that the independent entrepreneur is the ideal model, black Namibians are engaged in these schemes, not as entrepreneurs but as workers, and unskilled workers at that. They are under close white managerial control. On the Mangetti ranch the majority are apparently even without their families.[18] Production methods are wholly inappropriate for peasant farmers, and so provide little useful training. The schemes purchase few inputs locally, and sell the bulk of their non-cereal output outside the bantustans, or even to military camps. In reality, what the colonial regime chooses to call 'development' bypasses the Namibian peasantry altogether. Underdevelopment and impoverishment continue, and no remedy is provided for the effects of recent disasters.

4.5 The Impact of Drought and War in Peasant Areas

Black stockfarmers have been even more seriously affected by the recent drought than the settlers. The inferior pasture and groundwater have run out more quickly. Whereas in pre-colonial times at least part of the herds and flocks could be saved by scouring the interior for pockets of pasture and water, this is simply impossible in the marginal, overcrowded reserves. Very few farmers can afford to hire grazing or bring in fodder or water. Nor is it easy to sell the stock they cannot save, for marketing services remain rudimentary. By the time

---

17.   *Spectrum*, 2, 1-2, 3, (1980).
18.   *Rand Daily Mail* 24 April 1975, *Windhoek Observer* 17 April 1982.

Table 6

State Agricultural Schemes along the Okavango and Zambezi Rivers, 1978-9

	Okavango (west to east)				Zambezi	Total
	Musese	Vungu-Vungu	Shitemo	Shadikongoro	near Katima Mulilo	
Started production (date)	1977	1973	1978	?1975	1978/9	
Area cultivated (ha)	760	120	500	480	550	*2410*
Area irrigated (ha)	400	60	320	280	50	*1110*
Employment	n.a.	60	280	120[1]	60	*850*[2]

The data are approximate — even official sources do not always agree.

Notes
1. Reported as rising to 400 during the harvest.
2. A 1977 estimate for the Okavango schemes projected forward. There may be up to 500 additional seasonal jobs.

Sources
ELK 1976/7, pp.4-5; Stellenbosch 1980, pp.84-5; *SWA Annual 1977*, pp.59-61; press reports.

the central government allocated substantial funds to drought relief —
on average one-fortieth of the sum per household available to white
settlers — most livestock in the central and southern reserves were
already dead or dying.

By late 1981, most large and small stock in the southern reserves,
'Damaraland' and the Kaokoveld had perished. Many of the
inhabitants were reduced to destitution, and moved in desperation to
swell the ranks of the urban unemployed or to the bantustan
administrative centres. Extensive food shortages, malnutrition and
even deaths from starvation were reported from 'Damaraland' and
the Kaokoveld during 1981. Black stock-owners have survived the
destruction of most of their animals several times before in this
century, but recovery is a long and hard process. The poorer
households in particular may not be able to survive as farmers at all,
given the level of underdevelopment. Such resources as were provided
through DTA policy went for the most part not to them but to the 'big
men'.

The northern arable zone, containing most peasants, was
apparently not devastated to the same degree. Nevertheless it suffered
poor harvests, forcing increased reliance on wage income. There were
marked grain shortages in the Okavango valley and eastern Caprivi
Strip. The Ovambo canal system, designed to provide reliable water
supplies during droughts, apparently partly failed, for late in 1981 the
main feeder dam of the southern canal, the Olushandja, was reported
to be dry.[19] Happily, the 1982 season saw a good harvest in
Ovamboland.

In the north, however, the sufferings caused by the South African
repression of the national liberation movement have been added. The
overwhelming support of the civilian population for SWAPO has
been attested by many witnesses, including the South Africans
themselves.[20] Within the small pockets of peasant settlement in the far
north the SADF has located an intensity of concentration of personnel
and fire-power above anything seen in Zimbabwe and more akin to
Vietnam at the height of the American occupation.

Increasingly, this huge military machine has resorted to tactics of
terror. Some have been the random reactions of poorly motivated
conscripts and mercenaries in an unwinnable war — the beatings,
rapings and arbitrary killings to which blacks are vulnerable at any
time. Others are the result of deliberate military strategy: the

---

19.   *Windhoek Observer* 21 Nov, 5 Dec. 1981, cited in Hurlich 1982, p.292. The dam
      was reported only 17% full two months later (*Windhoek Observer* 13 Feb. 1982).
20.   This support and the response of the occupying forces is detailed in CIIR/BCC
      1981.

destruction of church schools and hospitals; the burning down of houses and crops near the scene of a guerrilla attack; the carefully planted mines and grenades which can then be blamed on PLAN; the SADF mercenary units which pillage and murder disguised as PLAN guerrillas; the rounding up of adult males, sometimes from whole districts at a time, for interrogation under torture in police or army detention camps; the detention and torture of those suspected of being SWAPO supporters or of refusing to inform on the movements of PLAN cadres.

Since 1977, and in Ovamboland since 1972, the north has been under virtual martial law, which today gives the security forces blanket powers of arrest, interrogation and detention, allows them complete legal immunity for any repressive act, imposes a dusk-to-dawn curfew on all inhabitants and lays down harsh penalties for failing to report guerrilla movements. Today martial law extends to much of central Namibia as well. Tens of thousands of peasants have been forced to take refuge in Angola and Zambia, and many others have left to join the forces of the liberation movement.

It goes without saying that agriculture too is a casualty of war, especially in Ovamboland. Production still continues — but subject to the curfew, destruction of crops in military manoeuvres and, it was reported by church sources in 1982, orders in some places not to work on the fields on two days each week, for fear that a plentiful harvest would be used to feed SWAPO guerrillas. SWAPO also reports that wells have been poisoned in the Kaokoveld in order to force the local stock-farmers to gather together under South African guard. Counter-insurgency is accelerating the disintegration of peasant society.

4.6 Women in Namibian Agriculture

The position of black women in rural society and in agricultural production today demands special consideration, although the almost complete lack of social data and the low political priority accorded to the issue makes extended discussion very difficult. As we have seen, the generally inferior position of women was perhaps the most systematic social cleavage in pre-colonial Namibian society. Colonial rule, and in particular the migrant labour system, has radically worsened their position, making women the most oppressed social group in present-day Namibia. An understanding of the form of that oppression is important for post-independence development policy, for its pervasive nature is easily downgraded in the overriding struggle for the ending of colonial rule and of gross class exploitation.

The deteriorating position of women in the rural areas during the colonial epoch has resulted partly from general legal discrimination. In the reserves, the South Africans imposed a repressive and artificial system of 'tribal law', which reduced women, whether married or single, to a legal status inferior to that of men. To enforce this system a subordinate, largely male administration of paid 'chiefs' and 'headmen' was created; some were collaborators from the old tribal order. They were given considerable local powers over the allocation of land and the adjudication of disputes, particularly in the northern reserves. As a result, with few exceptions, use-rights to land continue to be vested in male household heads. Most peasant women can survive only as subordinate members in the household of a husband or male relative, even if the latter is absent for long periods.

Discrimination has also arisen from social and economic custom. This is especially the case in wage employment, where women have been excluded from virtually all occupations except cleaning, domestic service and the lower grades of teaching and nursing. On the ranches, farmers have perpetuated the old exclusion of women from working with livestock; in 1970/71, 95% of regular and casual farmworkers were men, and the majority of the 5 000 women whose employment was recorded were house-servants (see Table 3). It is therefore almost impossible for most women to earn a cash income or to acquire industrial skills and experience.

The worsening plight of rural women under colonialism has been more than simply a legacy of the pre-colonial division of labour and a disadvantaged position in the competition for jobs. The main economic purpose of the migrant labour system was to keep wage rates down to a level below the subsistence requirements of a worker's family. It therefore compelled his wife to work both as a full-time mother and as a full-time agricultural producer at least partly supporting herself and the children and other dependants in the peasant household.

The differing degrees of involvement of women in agricultural production in the stock-raising and the arable reserves has been reflected in different experiences of migrant labour. In the former, where it appears that the pre-colonial exclusion of women from managing livestock has not radically altered, limited numbers of women have been able to move to the towns and farms, in a few cases as workers in their own right. The core of the system, however, has been the regime of contract labour applied to the peasantry of the northern mixed farming zone, where women have always undertaken most of the field cultivation and food processing. Throughout the SWANLA period (1926-72) an explicit sex bar was enforced: only men were recruited, and with very few exceptions only those with labour contracts were allowed to leave for the Police Zone where nearly all employment was located. Most women were, therefore, trapped in the reserves.

SWANLA served its exploitative role effectively, setting a scale of minimum wage-rates which few employers cared to exceed and which substantially undercut the prevailing rates for other black workers. Even when workers were able to save part of their wages, pay rates were so low that what they could send home could never cover all their families' needs. The position probably worsened between 1955 and 1970, as household food production provided for less and less of these needs. After the national strike of 1971/72, which led to the abolition of SWANLA, the wages of contract labourers were raised nearer to those of other black workers, and in the larger mines rates have improved considerably in real terms. This trend reflects the militancy of the workers but also the decreasing ability of peasant households to subsist from their own food production.

Nevertheless, the basis of migrant labour remains intact. It rests on the double exploitation of women's work on the land and in the home. First they are left with most of the responsibility for the task of child-rearing, which demands round-the-clock attention especially during infancy, and also for caring for the elderly, the sick and the disabled. In pre-colonial society, men had played a substantial if not equal part in these roles. At the same time women alone must now undertake the cultivation of the fields — with hand-tool technology a very labour-intensive occupation — and also the herding of stock, the organisation of the household economy and the repair of buildings and equipment.

They have little male assistance except for clearing new land, digging wells and herding cattle. Many of the younger contract workers can afford to spend only a few weeks at home between contracts of 6, 12 or 18 months' duration, and only occasionally a whole season. As a result, a considerable number of households may now go for long periods without any younger men resident at all. As underdevelopment has deepened and regular wage income from migrant labour or local government employment has become a necessity for most households, there has been a massive withdrawal of male labour from the peasant economy, above all in Ovamboland. Calculations based on the 1970 census and a 1974 sample survey suggest that in the adult population of rural Ovamboland between the ages of 15 and 59, women were 75% more numerous than men and made up nearly two-thirds of the total (see Table 7). This severe imbalance has probably worsened since then as the number of contract workers has increased, as unemployed men have moved to the towns, and as others have moved to join the liberation movement.

The never-ending arduous labour of peasant women was

59

Table 7

The Impact of Labour Migration on Household Structure in Ovamboland, 1970

Households[1]	Resident population aged 15-59				number of men per 100 women
	total		per household		
	men	women	men	women	
68 000	46 000	88 000	0.68	1.29	52

These figures are estimates only.

Notes
1. Here taken to average 5 individuals. This figure is arbitrary, for no reliable census has yet been taken. The number of family members and relatives per homestead will often be greater.

Sources
1970 Census; Stellenbosch 1978, Tables 3.1-5.

---

described in an interview in 1977 by a woman from the north:[21]

> . . . Apart from something like a one hour break at about 10 am to go for breakfast and to feed children, women in these areas work from 5 am to 1 pm from Monday to Saturday, every week. This is true whether you are talking about cultivation, weeding or harvesting seasons of the year . . . After spending up to 7 hours of backbreaking labour in the fields, women in the rural areas do not retire to rest for the day. They must also fetch water, grind grain into flour, and prepare meals, not to mention washing the babies . . .

The productive and caring roles regularly conflict, as when women have to spend many hours, particularly in the rainy season, taking sick children to distant clinics. On top of economic and social hardship comes the emotional suffering, shared equally by men, of long separations and the disruption of family life. Since the partial relaxation of the pass laws in 1977 some families have been reunited, but low wages, high unemployment, lack of family housing and systematic harassment by the police have prevented most women and children from joining their menfolk in the south.

These harsh conditions have nonetheless been the forcing-ground for the development amongst rural women of an awareness both of colonial repression in general and of their specific oppression in

---

21. Chicago Committee 1977, p.9.

particular. As contract labour and the war have removed husbands, brothers and sons, peasant women have taken an increasing role at all levels of decision-making — as organisers of field and stock production, as small traders, as educators, as members of social, church and political organisations, as defenders of local people against South African military harassment. As a result of such experience, women have increasingly come to insist that the transformation of their position become part of the process of liberation.

4.7 Agriculture in the Overall Economy

A hallmark of Namibia as a colony is the extent to which the sectors of the economy are linked to the outside world rather than integrated with each other. In the first place, Namibia is no longer self-sufficient in food; instead it is a market for South African farmers. Table A5 in the Appendix gives the detailed picture. By the early 1970s annual grain imports from South Africa averaged 27 000 tonnes of maize and maize products and 9 000 tonnes of wheat compared with total home production in years of good rainfall of perhaps 75 000 tonnes of grain (70% grown by the black peasantry). In drought, imports are much higher: 130 000 tonnes (including stock-feed) in 1970.[22] In fresh produce (dairy, vegetables and fruit) the imbalance is greater, although to what extent is unclear for lack of trade statistics.

It may be argued with some force that it is an efficient use of Namibia's natural resources to rear cattle and sheep for export, and import grain. This view, however, does no more than reflect a current balance of economic advantage and excludes other possible priorities in national development policy, such as self-reliance in food production and expanded employment in agriculture. The economic balance itself fluctuates. World beef prices vary, and are strongly influenced by powerful protectionist trading blocs such as the EEC; South African prices have been highly volatile in recent years, bringing Namibian ranchers windfall profits in times of scarcity but near to ruin in times of glut, as in the late 1970s. The balance is also partly artificial. First, it reflects the ability of the affluent — in southern Africa and world wide — to enforce their demand for meat over the need of the poor for meal and bread: the rich can afford to pay high prices for beef, and so farmers on marginal land find it more profitable to raise cattle than crops. Second, there is an in-built bias in South African farm and food subsidies. While South Africa keeps

---

22.   *SWA Survey* 1974, pp.34,36. See also Tables 5 and A5.

maize prices low in order to hold down wage costs, growers in Namibia do not get the compensating input subsidies handed out to their counterparts in South Africa. The heavy state capital subsidies — fencing, boreholes etc — also favour stock over arable farmers. These plus the pattern of land ownership generate a bias towards extensive, capital-intensive production methods, which in Namibian conditions suit stock-raising, even where intensive, labour-based methods, favouring cultivation, would be feasible ecologically and yield a higher return (properly costed) to the labour and capital invested.

A shortage of food affects the health of Namibians. Although the diseases of malnutrition are not yet widespread (as they are in the more devastated South African bantustans), they are not unknown and are accompanied more widely by other endemic diseases — TB and intestinal disorders — typically associated with poverty.

Most farm inputs are imported from South Africa. Similarly, few agricultural products are processed locally. Almost all tanning, dyeing and garment-making from karakul pelts is carried out overseas. Karakul wool is despatched in its raw state to South Africa, although 40% of its weight could be removed by scouring. According to a recent study a wool-scouring plant was closed down by the administration. A 1979 letter to the *Windhoek Advertiser* alleged that 'for a long time handweaving plants could not legally obtain their requirements directly in the Territory. In fact the local wool-washing plant cannot obtain raw wool directly here today.' Imposition of inappropriate hygiene methods appears to have accelerated the decline of butter and cheese production after the mid-1960s. A proportion of maize milling is carried out locally, but the last wheat mill closed in 1972.[23]

It is in Namibia's meat industry that the restrictions dictated by colonial self-interest have perhaps been most crippling. Between 1963 and 1976, three-quarters of cattle marketed for export were despatched live to South Africa. The purpose was to utilise spare South African slaughtering capacity, despite the cost to Namibian ranchers of the cattle losing condition during the journey, and of transport itself. Namibia's own meat processing capacity has been expanded only when drought has forced heavy sales at the same time as access to South Africa's markets has been restricted and sales outside South Africa therefore encouraged. During the early 1960s, when foot and mouth disease severely reduced cattle exports to South Africa, canneries were built at Okahandja and Otavi, and the

23.   Schneider-Barthold 1980, pp.107-8 note; *Windhoek Advertiser* 19 Sept. 1979; SWA Grain Board, *Annual Report* 1972, p.2.

Windhoek cannery and coldstore expanded. Apart from the Bantu Investment Corporation's prestige Eloolo cannery in Ovamboland, little further investment occurred until the 1977-80 crisis, when a large new processing plant was built at Gobabis. Export processing capacity (both cold storage and canning) was tripled to about 300 000 head per year — somewhat over 80% of Namibia's average annual exports (Table 8).

Once the plant is built, its use is still subordinated to South African needs. Cattle are still sent live to South Africa when profitable. Local slaughterings reached 155 000 head a year during the peak period of 1971-3 and 225 000 in 1980. However, they fell as low as 70 000 during 1973-4 and plummeted again during 1981, forcing

Table 8

The Meat Processing Industry

Location	Owner	Investment 1977-81 million rand	Cattle processing capacity head per day		Cattle processing capacity 000 head per annum	
			1977	1981	1977	1981
Windhoek	DMP	7.5	300	700	60	140
Otavi	DMP	3.1	150	300	30	60
Okahandja	KMP	4.7	200	400	40	80
Gobabis[1]	FNDC	13	—	400	—	80
Ranch sector total		*28.3*	*650*	*1800*	*130*	*360*
Oshakati[2]	FNDC	2	—	150	—	30
Total		*30.3*	*650*	*1950*	*130*	*390*

Companies
DMP — Damara Meat Packers (Vleissentraal, South Africa).
KMP — Karoo Meat Packers (South Africa).
FNDC— First National Development Corporation (South African government).

All figures are derived from press reports, not all of which are mutually consistent, and must therefore be treated with caution. All plants have abattoirs and canneries; all except Oshakati (and possibly Otavi) have or are planned to have chilling/freezing and cold storage facilities.

Notes
1. Reported in mid-1981 to be near completion but not yet operating.
2. Completed by 1977 but not apparently in operation until the latter part of that year.

Sources
Windhoek Observer 3 Mar., 1 Sept. 1979.
Windhoek Advertiser 19 Jul. 1977; 11 Aug. 1978; 6 Mar. 1979; 25 June 1980; 25 Jul. 1980: 1 Aug. 1980.
Rand Daily Mail 8 Mar. 1981.

the temporary closure of all except the Windhoek factory. For a time this had to go to the lengths of importing meat from Ireland in order to keep its cannery lines running.

The comparison with neighbouring Botswana, another major beef exporter, is striking. Botswana stopped almost all live exports in 1967 (the year after independence) and its state-owned processing plant has concentrated attention on refrigerated sales to the EEC — from whose high prices Namibia is excluded as a territory ineligible for Lomé Convention preferences. Botswana has sent a high proportion of exports to South Africa only when heavy competition or disease restricted access to Europe. It can also turn to third markets which South Africa has often denied Namibia.

Since 1977, a shift has occurred in South African strategy. The parastatal FNDC, in particular, has supported the Gobabis meat factory and an associated cold store at Walvis Bay (R1.5m), a venison factory (R1.6m) and maize mill (R0.5m) at Windhoek, and an oil-seed factory at Omaruru (R2.25m). Such investment, however, has much to do with entrenching free enterprise and foreign control of Namibia's resources after nominal independence. The Gobabis/ Walvis Bay project was launched in partnership with Socopo, a major French wholesale cooperative, which was to manage the Namibian plants and have first option on the factory's output. The venison factory is owned 50% by 'two West German businessmen'. And the oil-seed factory was built by South African in preference to local firms, takes its bulk supplies of sunflower seeds and oil from South Africa, and is part-owned and managed by the South African co-operative Boere Kooperatiewe Beperk (BKB), which has thereby secured a very useful market monopoly in cooking oil. South African businesses continue to own the meat factories, grain mills and bulk grain trade, and BKB has a 50% shareholding in one of the two international fur brokers concerned with karakul marketing.[24] The constraints on an independent Namibia are formidable.

---

24.   Eastwood and Holt Ltd. See also Table 8.

5 Independence and Agricultural Transformation

5.1 The Legacy of Colonialism and the Need for Radical Change

Namibian agriculture is today in deep crisis. The present appearance of that crisis is strongly coloured by the dramatic short-term impact of one of the worst droughts this century. By early 1982, many settler ranches except in the far east and north were bare of pasture and all but a residual core of breeding stock. In the small- and mixed-stock reserves the majority of the animals had died; in the north-west, very few were left alive at all. The large-stock and arable reserves, although apparently not quite so seriously affected, had suffered depleted pasture, stock losses and bad harvests. Throughout the stock-raising zones large numbers of peasants had been driven off the land in destitution, and a growing minority — as many as a fifth — of settler farmers had abandoned their ranches. Some of the damage may well be permanent. Economic hardship tends to strengthen the wealthy at the expense of the poor, and some of the marginal ranchers may not return. Destitute peasant stock-farmers, lacking the comprehensive financial and technical assistance lavished on the settlers, may find it impossible to survive any longer on the land, despite their proven tenacity and resourcefulness.

In 1982, the drought broke in the northern half of the country, and Ovamboland in particular reaped an excellent harvest. For the small-stock zone in the south, however, there was no respite. When normal rains do eventually return there may be an apparent agricultural recovery. But it may well be deceptive. Abundant pasture, rapidly rising numbers of stock, and returning farmers may mask the long-term acceleration of agrarian decline — overhasty restocking preventing the perennial grasses and shrubs from fully recovering; deepening peasant impoverishment on overcrowded and wasting land;

the polarisation between the affluent and the marginal amongst the settler farmers.

Nor will normal rainfall eliminate other long-term problems. South African meat prices are highly volatile; karakul pelt prices are likely to continue low in a depressed world economy. The increasing capital intensity of production methods on commercial farms and development projects reduces the scope for creating desperately needed employment. Heavy dependence on expensive imported inputs remains. So does the domination of the South African market for slaughter stock, despite the installation of extra processing capacity; the steady supplies required by Namibian meat factories will always be disrupted when South African prices and quotas for cattle on the hoof are high, encouraging Namibian ranchers to divert their cattle to South African abattoirs. South African control of food and stock-feed imports also remains total, leaving Namibian agriculture and nutrition at the mercy of South African economic and political manipulation.

In short, for all the cosmetic tinkering with the institutions and the language of government, the core structure of colonial exploitation persists unchanged. Less than 5 000 ranchers — now including a few black faces — own over 80% of all good stock-raising land while 20 000 stock-farming peasant households are left with the remaining 20%; 120 000 arable peasant households are compressed into just 5% of total viable farmland in the far north. The migrant labour system, although legally more flexible, continues to be driven by the relentless engine of rural impoverishment. On top of all this is the growing disruption of both peasant and commercial farming caused by war.

There are three fundamental arguments for radical change in Namibian agriculture. The first is that the present combination of over-intensive, profit-motivated commercial ranching and over-crowded, impoverished peasant farming is seriously damaging the ecological base of the agricultural economy, and will continue to do so as long as the present distribution and use of the land remains substantially unchanged. The second is that neither sector is efficient by normal socio-economic standards. The large commercial ranches do not earn a plausible return on capital even with state subsidies and minimal wages. The peasant sector, although relatively productive given its lack of resources and low technology, cannot provide even basic subsistence for most of the overcrowded population which works its fields and pastures.

The third is that both sectors of Namibian agriculture exhibit an extreme form of colonial exploitation, in peasant agriculture through the migrant labour system, in commercial farming through the labour

66

of a repressed workforce on starvation wage rates. A whole structure of social and political injustice has been erected over Namibian peasants and farmworkers: the denial of participation and democratic control in the economic and political organisations which order every aspect of their lives; authoritarian and racist treatment; lack of skills and access to appropriate technology; high unemployment; the enforced break-up of families; lack of basic social security services; and, above all, grinding poverty. Radical restructuring of both peasant and commercial agriculture is needed in order to achieve even modest improvements in human and political rights.

5.2 Context and Priorities

Any attempt to predict economic and social trends in the Namibian agricultural sector and to discuss rural development strategy is faced with special difficulties. In the first place, the likely situation at independence is far from clear. An agreed transition to independence is not yet in sight, nor is there hard evidence that South Africa has any specific target date in view. 'Independence' therefore has a time horizon of anything between 1983 and some point in the indefinite future. The longer the interval, the more speculative become any extrapolations from the patterns of the recent past, particularly because central features of the old colonial order are now beginning to crumble. It is not possible simply to freeze the present and transfer it without qualification to some future threshold of independence.

Secondly, the terms of independence, whenever it comes, will clearly make a great deal of difference to both the short and the long-term aftermath. Namibia's economic, social and administrative structures have been so closely integrated into those of the Republic that any thorough-going disengagement is bound to be a radical process. Thirdly, the resources on which an incoming Namibian government will be able to count in framing and carrying through its development programme will depend in part on the level of international solidarity it is able to engage. This will be strongly influenced by regional and global shifts in the balance of economic and political forces generally. Fourthly, the attention of the liberation movement and of Namibians generally has been more urgently engaged by the demands of the liberation struggle than by the detailed formulation of future development strategy. It is obviously the right of Namibians to decide that strategy, and it will be moulded by experience in the course of that struggle. On both counts, it is not appropriate to advocate specific policies from outside.

For all these reasons, hypothetical detail about an uncertain future would be unhelpful here. It would be more useful to outline the constraints and opportunities implied by the preceding analysis of the unjust structures of the past. Nevertheless, any analysis of past colonial oppression implies future preferred alternatives, however strongly qualified by uncertainty and the lack of essential information. If debate about agrarian development after independence is to be encouraged, these preferences need to be made explicit. Yet they cannot be stated abstractly, assuming away both the legacy of the past and political conditions after independence. It is essential to assess the context of future policy — the range of probable scenarios which may confront the Namibian government and people.

The first crucial element of this context is that observers are agreed that SWAPO commands popular support nationwide, and, barring an unforeseen and serious reverse, it will form the independence government. The party's basic principles and policy objectives therefore command attention, and its detailed statements on agriculture are examined below. Most importantly, SWAPO is committed to a transition to socialism, though it believes this will be a long and arduous process. 'Development' therefore does not mean a simple pursuit of economic growth, which would only strengthen the present structures. The 'non-exploitative and non-oppressive classless society' envisaged by SWAPO clearly presupposes a broader concept of development in which positive action by the party and the state is called for to transform the present race- and class-divided society, and to eliminate mass poverty. This is seen as a continuous struggle, to which rural development, whatever its internal priorities, is integrally related.

The second element in the context of future policy is the prospect that, barring a major delay in the timing of independence, Namibian agriculture will arrive at the threshold of independence with its present framework fundamentally intact. While South African rule continues, the present division of the land into commercial and residual peasant sectors is likely to be preserved with only minor changes. In the bantustans the slow marginalisation of subsistence agricultural production, already far advanced, will continue. The slight relaxation of the pass laws may allow a minority of migrant workers and their families to move permanently out of the bantustans, but urban unemployment and government restrictions on housing — the new face of 'influx control' — will keep the core of the migrant labour system in operation and force most bantustan inhabitants to remain on the land despite mass impoverishment.

On the other hand, inequality within peasant society is likely to increase only slowly. Recent DTA policies in the bantustans may increase the number and wealth of the few moderately large-scale black stock-farmers there. But because many of those who hold office in the bantustan governments depend on tribalist methods of control over communal land for their political influence with the South African administration, neither private land ownership nor outright landlessness are likely to expand rapidly. If there is a mass flight from the land, it will probably be the result of an escalation of terror tactics by the South African military in the northern bantustans.

In the commercial sector, while it is difficult to assess the long-term consequences of the post-1974 crisis, ranchers are leaving: the white civilian population of Namibia fell from 90 000 in 1970 to 76 000 in the 1981 census. Nevertheless a wholesale abandonment of settler ranches does not yet appear to be under way. The recent admission of black Namibians to the resettlement programme amounts to little more than a very limited sharing of the spoils of the original land theft with a few political collaborators and well-off stock-farmers, neither of whom are numerous. On the other hand, there are long-term structural tendencies towards the ecological degradation of the pasture, the concentration of ownership in fewer hands, the drift from the land of the younger and poorer rather than the older, well-established farming families, the shift of residence from farm-house to town suburb, and the transfer of profits to South Africa or to non-farming purposes. These all continue the gradual reshaping of traditional settler farming into a core of larger-scale stock-ranching businesses, perhaps with an increasing proportion of company ownership, and a sizeable periphery of individual farmers struggling to maintain their affluent lifestyle and depending on extensive state and commercial credit.

Perhaps the most important unknown factor is the extent to which PLAN will be able to extend its operations and to disrupt ranching in central and southern Namibia. Already in the northern half of the cattle-ranching zone, where PLAN cadres have been continuously active for more than five years, there has been a substantial breakdown of colonial authority and a general flight of white farmers, leaving a large minority of farms abandoned or in de facto possession of black farm-workers, peasants or DTA clients.

With this agrarian framework largely intact, the terms of the independence settlement will be critical. The direction of post-independence rural development policy will hinge upon the extent to which the incoming Namibian government can win the freedom to implement its declared political commitment to the ending of injustice, inequality and exploitation. Justice demands that land and the fruits of the land be far more widely shared than at present. If the independence constitution is formulated solely by the representatives of the Namibian people, as presently envisaged by UN resolutions governing the transition process, then it will be possible to frame the legal instruments which will facilitate a just restructuring of Namibian agriculture. If however, the constitution entrenches the ownership of land and the principal means of production, as well as the civil service, in settler hands, then the capacity of the post-independence state to effect rapid and fundamental change may be severely limited. This would be less the case in the former reserves, for the development of which acceptable international aid should be readily available, than in the commercial sector: the transformation of settler ranches on any scale might then prove a complicated, piecemeal, lengthy and expensive process. Aid donors are unlikely to be forthcoming with finance for compensation; and nationalisation of land without immediate compensation would risk economic retaliation by departing ranchers, by South Africa, and possibly by Western aid donors.

In practice, the two alternative scenarios sketched above — independence with full freedom of action or independence with entrenched protection for private privilege — are likely to converge in important respects. In the case of the first, any rapid and unilateral extension of social ownership and control might well provoke the destruction of buildings, machinery and breeding stock by departing ranchers. Damaging reprisals could be expected from South Africa, and, if government action went beyond ranching, also from the mining companies and their Western protectors. So great is Namibia's trade dependence and so powerful are foreign companies in the commercial economy that the severity of the short-term impact of such reprisals would prejudice the long-term objectives of the reforms.

A post-independence Namibian government is therefore likely to proceed with caution, however great its theoretical freedom to act. This is in fact implicitly recognised by SWAPO in its clear statement of commitment to radical social change and equally clear avoidance of specifying precise means and timings. On the other hand, a continuation of the extreme inequalities and injustices of colonial society with only minor reforms would so manifestly fail to meet popular expectations forged in decades of suffering and struggle that a SWAPO government would face mounting popular discontent. Popular pressure, including land occupation, would render ineffective clauses in the constitution which clearly stood in the way of social justice. Indeed, if the international community wishes stability in Namibia, it would be unwise as well as immoral to impose terms for independence which so froze the unjust structures of the past.

Perhaps the most formidable constraint facing the new government will be the extremely limited resources of skilled people available. For the country as a whole, there were in 1977 only about 5 000 Africans who had received secondary school education inside Namibia. 93% of managerial and professional jobs were held by whites. SWAPO's external training effort, with some 3 000 secondary school and 500 post-secondary school enrolments in 1981, will be significant. But it still has to be set against the 18 000 high and middle level people employed in 1977 within the civil service alone.[1] Specialist agricultural skills are in even shorter supply. There seems to be no government agricultural extension service in Ovamboland, for example. Both ranchers and technical officers in the various agricultural departments are white, and many may leave after independence. The Agricultural School at Ogongo in Ovamboland — one of only two for black Namibians — has apparently produced only a handful of graduates from its three-year course since it opened in 1973, and in 1982 it had only 20 trainees in all; three of the seven teachers there are South African soldiers in uniform. In total contrast, the Neudamm Agricultural College for whites takes about 60 students a year and has a training staff of 15; by 1978 it had produced 447 graduates since its opening in 1956.[2]

Priorities
The principal implication of this skill shortage is the need of the incoming government to concentrate resources singlemindedly on key issues if transformation is to be achieved. So much cries out for change in Namibian agriculture that it would be easy to spread resources thinly to try to meet all demands. If this were done, however, the opportunity for fundamental changes might be missed. Any thorough-going changes require major inputs of skill. They would mean concentrating skilled people (and training programmes) on specific tasks, rather than spreading them out. The government would need to isolate the issues of highest priority and concentrate on them. Perhaps more difficult, it would have to identify issues of low priority (however desirable) and deny resources to them. It might not be too much to say, for example, that Namibia could recruit enough skilled people in the first five years *either* to organise a major land reform in the present settler ranching zone, *or* to extend cattle raising and cultivation in the sandveld fringe, but not both, since each would need heavy inputs of advisory, credit, marketing and technical skills. This particular dilemma may not arise in practice — the detailed research and planning has not yet been done — but it illustrates the

---

1. On skills and manpower generally, see UNIN 1978, also Green & Kiljunen 1981, Tables 6-12.
2. Melber 1979, pp.118-9.

kind of difficult choices that will arise. So too does the experience of Zimbabwe, where, despite having far more skilled people at its disposal, the government's land reform programme has been held back by lack of suitably trained staff.

5.3 The Aftermath of Independence

The immediate short-term issues facing the new government will depend on the timing of independence: a threshold of 1983, for example, would mean tackling all the consequences of the current agricultural slump. However, whatever the date, the short-term problems may be formidable, and the manner of their resolution will strongly influence the shape of longer-term rural development policy.

The problems will be less acute in the peasant areas, where few settler and foreign-owned assets are directly involved. Most households will still have some stake in agricultural production and will require few inputs to be able to continue to produce. Meeting the food deficit of these areas will take a relatively minor proportion of total food imports, though it will still be a major logistical exercise if the retreating South Africans deny port and railway facilities at Walvis Bay.

Inextricably related will be the effect of the run-down of the migrant labour system. Movements of population into and out of the peasant sector will be difficult either to regulate or to reverse. The return of tens of thousands of war refugees is likely to be outweighed by the exodus of underemployed men and the families of migrant workers to seek jobs and housing in the towns, mines and ranches. In view of workers' long experience of desperate urban unemployment and overcrowding, the pace and scale of the exodus caused by the reuniting of families may be less than anticipated in a recent UNIN study.[3] Some migrant workers or their families may not wish to abandon their stake in agriculture entirely and a number will continue to retire to the land later in life. Nevertheless the flow to town will be large, and urban provision will severely tax the resources of the state.

Government urban policy, especially towards wages and housing, will have important repercussions on peasant agriculture. The higher wages and urban social spending rise in relation to rural incomes and basic services, the greater will be the incentive for people to leave an impoverished and (in the north) war-damaged peasant sector. At the same time the state resources available to support the peasant sector from the very limited pool of personnel, finance and organisational

---

3.   UNIN 1978, pp.17-8.

capacity will be correspondingly less.

The effect on agriculture itself of an exodus to town from the rural areas will cut two ways. Permanent migration of whole households would reduce pressure on land, pasture, water and wood and so make an initial rise in average household incomes, including cash earnings from sales of produce, somewhat easier. On the other hand, the sudden drop in remittances from migrant workers who have moved away permanently would deepen the impoverishment of people who depend on them now, including both relatives who receive money directly, and also people who depend on the flow of money into the rural areas, such as part-time small traders, many of whom are women.

The scale of the rural exodus can be affected by state action, although only to a limited extent in the short term. One important measure to raise peasant cash incomes, particularly in the face of drought, would be to extend greatly the regular buying and transport of slaughter stock from the peasant areas to the abattoirs. The provision of improved services such as education and health will be vital but will take time — though some aspects such as an adult literacy campaign or rehabilitation of services cut by war (for example spraying to prevent malarial mosquitoes in Ovamboland) may be quicker. Raising crop prices would have rather little effect in most peasant areas since only a small proportion of harvest is marketed. More imaginative schemes to support crop incomes, such as subsidy of agricultural inputs or of on-farm grain storage deserve study. The difficulty will be to identify a scheme which does not require more staff and/or technical knowledge than immediately available at independence.

Another important issue will be to secure export markets, particularly if South Africa is hostile. The key market for beef is the EEC, with prices generally well above world levels. Negotiation of an EEC quota could be considered before independence. With the new abattoir capacity Namibia will be able to chill, freeze or can to EEC standards over 80% of its current output of beef cattle, which should suffice. Other markets could also be important: Africa (including Angola), the Middle and Far East, and Eastern Europe.

The present market outlook for karakul is grim. Joint marketing with other fur producers is a long-term possibility. As a holding operation, either or both of the two existing international brokers could probably be contracted to collect pelts, in addition to sorting and marketing. Meanwhile, it would be well to research alternative or additional products for the small-stock zone — ideally products which are less dependent on the volatile fashion whims of the very rich. The options are probably limited to wool, mohair and meat, involving a partial conversion from karakul to other breeds of sheep and to goats. Southern ranchers are in immediate need of a market for mutton from slaughtered karakul stock. Closure of the present South African market would be serious, as access to foreign countries may prove both difficult to negotiate and unprofitable. Expansion of local consumption of mutton would have the additional advantage of improving nutrition, but it would be unlikely to absorb anything like the total supply. Subsidiary products might include goat's milk and cheese, which have export possibilities.

Transport may pose a thorny problem, particularly if South Africa obstructs use of the railway, and the railway-owned lorry fleet, and Walvis Bay port. The details have been examined elsewhere:[4] here it suffices to note that airfreight and emergency work at Swakopmund harbour, together with emergency imports of railway equipment and especially refrigerated lorries could support a limited export of chilled beef and karakul pelts, and import of food. An adequate internal transport system is essential both for food supply and to encourage farmers to produce for sale.

5.4 Crisis and Transformation in Ranching

The crisis
The largest immediate crisis is likely to be over the settler ranches. It is also the most fundamental, for it goes to the heart of the present structure of Namibian society, and the unjust division of the land.

The commercial sector is very vulnerable to disruption at independence. The present mode of cattle and karakul ranching requires expensive inputs of stockfeed, implements and machinery, veterinary services, transport and marketing organisation. It also depends on skilled range management, particularly of pasturing and breeding. All these have hitherto been monopolised by South African suppliers, the colonial state, and white farmers and farm managers. Were they to be abruptly withdrawn, commercial ranching would be in crisis in a matter of weeks or months. Even with careful planning and advance funding it would not be possible to fill the gap in the short term: foreign experts would not have the essential detailed local knowledge and experience to maintain anything like current levels of production.

It seems likely that considerable disruption will in fact occur, even if the incoming government offered substantial inducements to have the system maintained. South African government co-operation

---

4.   In FAO 1982.

in any transitional arrangement cannot be relied upon. Many settlers may be unwilling to remain after independence at any price. They have an easy alternative: unlike Kenya in 1963, Namibia has an open border between colony and colonial ruler (South Africa), offering a safe haven for the transfer of assets, monetary or physical, right up to the moment of independence. Such transfers took place in Mozambique, Angola, and to a lesser degree, Zimbabwe. The majority of ranchers are first or second generation Afrikaners, nurtured in the belief that any concession to black nationalism is a betrayal of the white race. They are bitterly hostile even to the veneer of multi-racialism represented by the DTA, and many already have relatives or business interests in South Africa itself. The German minority of ranchers seem somewhat more likely to be willing to stay as owners or managers in an independent African state, if only for lack of an easy alternative.

The implication is that if the government wishes to keep most ranchers it will have to offer very large inducements. Yet the independence government, even if it wanted to, would clearly be unable to freeze matters as they are. Substantial numbers of Namibian farmworkers and residents of the central/southern reserves would be unwilling to accept perpetuation of the colonial land theft and the extreme exploitation which continued occupation of the land by white ranchers would represent. A double-edged spontaneous response would rapidly become evident, some moving out of farm employment altogether, others, as currently in Zimbabwe, taking over privately-owned land, whether abandoned or ostensibly settler-run.

Unplanned land occupation would lead to the problem of competing claimants for the land. The present permanent ranch workers would expect land. So too would the overcrowded residents of the present reserves. Some of these in the Police Zone reserves may claim historic rights where they are descendants of the pre-colonial clan and communal users of the land in a district; however, given the semi-migratory nature of cattle-keeping before the German occupation, specific families are unlikely to identify with specific plots. Contract workers from the north, where they remain in farm employment, are tending to settle permanently with their families at their place of work and would form a third group. There are also, particularly in the south, mobile teams of casual workers, often performing skilled tasks such as shearing or fence building. Without clear guidelines from the government, there is a real risk of conflict between these different claimants.

Keeping a maximum of existing settlers in place would carry a high economic and political price. Ranching would have to be made very clearly profitable in the short term: given that both beef and

75

karakul depend on export markets with world prices low at present, this would probably mean both substantial price subsidies (especially if EEC access for beef was not available) and continued low wages for farmworkers. Almost certainly guarantees would have to be given of immediate compensation on favourable valuations for any land taken over by the state, even if it was unoccupied and unused and despite the palpable injustice of the original land theft. Politically, preserving the settlers would mean substantial South African control over marketing, supplies and expert services, and continued subservience of farmworkers.

Is it worth paying this price to maintain the present system for a transitional period — even supposing the settlers would stay? The answer depends on the long-term view. Immediate decisions will have far-reaching consequences, and here it seems essential that a clear choice of long-term policy be worked out, preferably in advance of the transition period.

The implications of retaining present state agricultural personnel and related technical staff are somewhat different. They are at least as crucial as the ranches themselves. Again, it is likely that the Afrikaner expatriates will leave before or soon after independence. The question is how many of the territorially-born settler (including German) majority in these services will be willing to stay, and on what terms and conditions. They would need to be given contracts at or near their present real incomes, which would mean at levels well above any new unitary salary scale applicable to new state employees. However, they would presumably be willing to support land ownership and rural organisation patterns which differed from those of present white ranching.

Long-term options

The continuation of a substantially intact settler ranching sector would run directly counter to both the expectations of Namibians and any concept of development as benefiting the people as a whole. Many aspects are unacceptable — authoritarian work relationships, lack of participation in decision-making, low wages, rudimentary housing and facilities, and capital-intensive production methods. It would condemn most Namibians to the old colonial reserves, denying them the use of the bulk of the area of the country.

This is clearly also the view of SWAPO. The 1976 Political Programme opposes the division of Namibian agriculture into commercial settler-owned and residual peasant sectors. Specifically it envisages 'a comprehensive agrarian transformation aimed at giving the land to the tiller' as part of a programme of economic reconstruction which has 'as its motive force the establishment of a classless society. Social justice and progress for all is the governing idea behind every SWAPO decision'. This theme of uniting all Namibians, especially peasants and workers, to build a non-exploitative society is one of SWAPO's principal stated objectives.

Much the same arguments would apply to an attempt simply to substitute Namibians for departing settlers and keep the structure intact, as has been done to some extent in Kenya or Zambia. The creation of a favoured class of black capitalist stock-farmers would run directly counter to basic goals of equality, participation and social justice. It would arouse vigorous opposition from excluded peasants and from farm-workers subordinated to new black 'baases', with a real risk of violent class and communal conflict. In any case, it is impossible that it could succeed as a short-term policy to maintain present production levels and techniques on the ranches. Bantustan policy has meant there are not individual black Namibians with the capital, or the detailed skill (especially in stock-breeding for karakul, and in botany for sophisticated and intensive camp rotation systems), to substitute one-for-one for departing settlers.

In the long term there are definite disadvantages to applying in the present ranching zone the 'peasant' cattle-keeping systems of the present 'reserves'. DTA experience shows that in the absence of communal control, turning over small numbers of ranches to cattle-owners overcrowded in the present reserves can lead to rapid destruction of the pasture as cattle flood on to the land. The well-known 'problem of the common' arises: when each person owns only a small number of the cattle grazing on a particular area, it is not in his interest to keep down the number of beasts he brings on; the pasture will only be conserved if *all* agree to prevent overgrazing. Likewise, it seems that pasture is best used if the whole herd is managed as one unit, rather than many different groups of animals moving separately. This may also be more equitable: in countries such as Botswana where individuals graze cattle on communal land a trend develops in which a few individuals accumulate large herds, while poorer people are forced to sell when emergencies arise. Wide disparities thus emerge.

There is no option in a pastoral zone for the kind of peasant land reform familiar from Kenya or Latin America, where large crop farms are divided into small plots, one for each household. With variable rainfall and the need to provide water points, cattle must be herded over large areas. It would not be feasible simply to divide up each ranch into family plots. The long-term alternative most consistent both with both equity and economic and ecological efficiency would appear to be some form of social ownership in the ranching sector. There are a variety of possible methods ranging from state farms through co-operatives to individual families with their own herds agreeing on joint use of communally-owned land. It is by no means obvious which form of organisation would be most appropriate to Namibian conditions and development objectives. SWAPO's Political Programme implies a flexible approach, at least initially, referring to 'peasant co-operatives or collectives' as well as 'state-owned ranching and crop farms'.

There is little directly comparable experience on which to draw because in most other ex-colonies with sizeable settler farming sectors, notably Kenya and Zimbabwe, the farms have been at least partly arable, allowing them, if converted to small-scale farming, to provide the bulk of their subsistence requirements from their own production. In the purely pastoral zone of central and southern Namibia this is simply not possible: farmers must sell livestock products in order to buy food and essential supplies. It is also physically and socially easier to devise workable forms of social ownership for cultivated land than for livestock. For example, cattle ranching is much less labour-intensive than crop growing; so if a number of small family herds are brought together, there are unlikely to be full-time jobs looking after the joint herd for all the family members who want them.

Group or co-operative ranches elsewhere in Africa have not been a notable success in terms of production — though for example in Kenya they have succeeded in preventing land being concentrated in the hands of the wealthy to the detriment of the people as a whole. One perhaps useful precedent in Namibia is the farm at the Catholic mission of Epukiro (north of Gobabis) where 10 000 hectares complete with water and fenced camps has been transferred to the control of the local village of about 100 households. They have elected a council to control the farm, and all cattle (to a maximum of 30 per household) are managed as one unit, with a total herd of about 1 000 head. The council employs four men full-time as part of the labour force, maintaining water-points and looking after the cattle. There is also a separate herd owned by the council, purchased with a grant from an outside aid agency, whose income is used to help pay running costs on the ranch. Clearly Epukiro has special features which cannot be reproduced on other ranches, and the employment it provides is limited — many villagers still migrate to work elsewhere. It might nevertheless be a useful model especially as the nearby mission is already running short courses in agriculture for farmers from other parts of Namibia.

Whatever form of ownership is decided on, there are also related questions about the most efficient size of production unit for cattle rearing. The present size of ranches arose largely from political rather than economic considerations — the need to settle a maximum number of white farmers at their accustomed standard of living. Some

78

authorities suggest that smaller ranches are more efficient than large, because more attention can be given to the herd on smaller farms and they are less complex to organise. On the other hand, the amalgamation of a number of ranches into larger units would permit an alternative form of pasture management: moving cattle greater distances in response to variations in rainfall and pasture conditions, in a modern version of the pre-colonial system. One possible pattern would be to retain the ranch as the unit of management, but also to establish an organisation embracing a number of ranches. This might provide marketing services and technical advice. It could also control areas of reserve grazing, or alternatively provide an agreed and controlled mechanism for allowing stock to be moved, in years of uneven rainfall, from ranches with low rainfall to those with more. There would be obvious advantages if such organisations were co-operatively owned by the ranches they covered.

Likewise there is a question-mark over the method of cattle-keeping. Pasture management is obviously crucial. Yet the present pattern of controlled grazing using fenced camps and boreholes is in fact a highly intensive method of land-use in semi-arid and arid conditions, and demands sophisticated and highly disciplined techniques of range management if profits are to be made and if the fragile vegetation is not to suffer. The majority of settlers have manifestly failed to provide management of adequate quality, for all the expert advice they have received: even South African officials acknowledge damage to the pasture. With expertise thinly spread and few Namibians experienced in management as opposed to supervision, a post-independence concentration on intensive rotational methods of range management throughout the ranching sector could prove ecologically damaging as well as financially expensive. An incoming government may wish to experiment in some areas with less skill-intensive methods requiring fewer (and so less costly) inputs, which still maintain the pasture. These might require a smaller number of beasts per hectare than ranching today, and so would be easier to introduce if the national herd is already reduced in numbers because of drought, as in 1982. Such a method would not necessarily be less profitable than ranching: in one striking study, Carvalho suggested that even 'traditional' methods of cattle-keeping in Southern Angola (just north of Namibia) were in some ways as efficient as ranching in colonial Zimbabwe.[5] Experiment would clearly be needed. Less intensive methods might be particularly appropriate in any new areas in the north opened for stock rearing by provision of water-points (see pp.84-85 below).

---

5.   Carvalho 1974, pp.222-4.

Which particular forms of ownership and production methods are promoted should depend on the relative priorities assigned to the principal rural development objectives, especially increased productivity, improved standards of living for the rural population, expanded rural employment (to reduce the rise in urban unemployment), and democratic participation in the production process. The interplay of these are examined in detail in the UNIN Agrarian Reform publication, and in the recent study by Chambers and Green.[6] The choices themselves are of course the prerogative of the representatives of the Namibian people. It seems almost certain, though, that the long-term goal will be some form of social ownership; experiment with several different approaches is likely. The lesson of experience elsewhere is the vital importance of local consultation and participation, of careful planning, and of adequate supporting services.

Transitional arrangements in ranching

If these long-term priorities were to be adopted, it is clear that they offer no reason to maximise the number of existing settlers who stay. It might nevertheless be argued that an initial effort should be directed to maintaining efficient production on as much of the ranch sector as possible. The aim would be to obtain, during the transitional phase, a large volume of exports — hence valuable foreign currency and taxable profits — and to avoid a forced flow of families from collapsing ranches to urban areas. The scheme would probably depend on a judicious mix of three elements: financial incentives to acceptable settlers, placing competent Namibians on abandoned ranches, perhaps under lifetime leasehold, and maintaining the existing framework of support services, replacing departing staff with foreign experts.

The first disadvantage of such a scheme is that it moves in the opposite direction of the long-term goal. The second is that it would be costly, both in money and in skilled personnel. The two disadvantages combined would mean that the state was committing a considerable proportion of its extremely scarce initial pool of skills and funds to rebuilding a sector that would still have some of the worst features of colonial farming. Work relationships would be unchanged, and ranch revenues would be unlikely to allow substantial improvement in family wages and living conditions.

On close examination, even the gains of such a scheme prove somewhat illusory. Agricultural exports are normally relatively unimportant (15-20% of visible exports) compared with minerals.

---

6. UNIN 1979; Chambers and Green 1981.

They would be more significant if mineral markets stay as depressed as in 1982, but it might also be difficult to find profitable agricultural markets soon after independence. As for the prospect of surplus from ranching, it was shown in an earlier chapter that, when properly costed, only the most efficient ranching enterprises yield profits, and that under present conditions, the sector as a whole is kept afloat by government subsidies. It would seem unwise, therefore, to devote a major part of government's scarce capacity to shoring up or rebuilding a relatively unchanged ranching sector. Furthermore, temporary deferment of structural reforms might only complicate their eventual implementation. There is a risk that deferment would in any case be no more successful in preventing a collapse when the time for implementation arrived.

This is not to say that the entire ranch sector can be immediately reformed, or production allowed to collapse. The government would not have the resources to carry out a sudden complete reform, nor, if ranches are abandoned en masse by the settlers, fully to maintain the incomes of all farm workers, or to keep the desirable core of breeding stock alive. In practice a number of white farmers may remain throughout the transition period and perhaps beyond. Their ranks will have been augmented before independence by black Namibian owners or leaseholders, for whom special arrangements may be necessary. This will certainly be the case with the black farmers of the Rehoboth Gebiet, which, although the poor relation of settler farming, is part and parcel of the privately-owned ranching sector and therefore of its exploitation of black workers. But, even in the transitional period, the government may well wish to direct its main focus elsewhere.

If it is decided that the long-term goal is broader participation in ranching through some kind of social ownership, then the immediate needs are likely to be (i) careful planning, (ii) encouraging participation and consultation of both present and potential ranch residents, (iii) starting a range of experimental schemes, and (iv) creating support services specifically geared to assist and expand the programme. Technical advice (especially on range management), advice on organisation of co-operatives and/or state farms, marketing, veterinary and water supply maintenance services must all be simple to understand and readily available. Existing staff would need retraining; courses would be needed to upgrade the skills of ranch residents. It would probably also be wise to concentrate training on new cadres of para-technical staff with the specific skills needed for particular tasks: they should require considerably shorter training than the alternative of fully qualified officers with generalised agricultural knowledge over a wide field. Such training might best be linked to experimental schemes, where students can 'learn by doing'

81

under careful supervision.

Foreign expertise would inevitably be required, with industrialised countries not necessarily the best source. It would be more important to offer inducements to acceptable members of the existing support services to stay than to settlers: veterinary and other officers who know local conditions are very valuable. However, it might also be worth offering generous compensation to those settlers who first upgrade their workers in management and technical skills, and who transfer equipment and breeding stock intact when they leave. Individual remaining settlers who are acceptable might also be contracted in various training roles.

A successful transformation will almost certainly require a slower initial pace than farm workers or overcrowded reserve residents would like. However, if a far-reaching programme is announced at the start, if consultation, planning and training are clearly visible, and if implementation is prompt, efficient and accelerating, popular support is likely. The alternative, spreading resources too thinly in a crash programme, risks failure. Indeed, if a large proportion of ranches are immediately abandoned (and especially if they are sabotaged), it might be most successful to concentrate the transformation programme initially on the most suitable group of these ranches; meanwhile the remainder could be occupied in an agreed way by peasant-owned herds.

The question remains as to what the transformation programme could consist of, in the short term. Perhaps the most promising for many abandoned ranches, even in the transitional period, would be production co-operatives of present workers and their families. This possibility turns on the fact that present ranch workers are used to working as a team, and their more senior members are de facto foremen already, especially on the large number of ranches visited at most fortnightly by their owners. Support services and training — particularly in how to handle the rotation of herds — would of course be needed. In this case all training and support costs would need to be borne by the state, as well as capital grants, especially toward housing and water development for spot irrigation. This would allow all ranch income to be put towards improving wages, maintaining capital assets, and rebuilding herds, which, given the 1978-81 drought and losses during the transition, may be below half levels in the 1970s. With small initial herds and adequate range management advice, it should be possible to avert serious and widespread range degradation.

Under these circumstances, incomes should be high enough to prevent mass exodus. The new cooperative work relationships would probably be different enough for popular enthusiasm to be mobilised, and technical advice to be accepted. Exports would fall, if only whilst local meat consumption is increased and herds rebuilt, but the base for their recovery would remain. The sector would still operate at a deficit, but with the operating subsidy borne by the state and financed from taxes on mining surpluses and with the main beneficiaries being Namibians working and living on the ranches. The key potential gains would be to create acceptable standards of living and work relationships, and to preserve the ranching sector in a way that laid the foundation for long-term development. The first such ranches would form the necessary base to permit experiments, and from which to expand.

The approach is not foolproof. It would be subject to high risks of settler sabotage, mistakes by imperfectly trained workers, and insufficient supporting services. It would also be expensive in terms of state support. But it looks more likely than the alternatives to be consistent with the long-term objectives of socially just work relationships, efficiency in production and conservation of natural resources.

5.5 The Long-Term Framework

Discussion of ranching has inevitably shifted the focus to the long term, and it remains to assess in more general terms the major constraints and possibilities for rural development strategy. Even in a climate as harsh as Namibia's, the technical possibilities for increased production are considerable, particularly through the opening up of presently under-utilised areas. However, these technical options can only be potential means of achieving economic, social and political goals. Of these, the elimination of economic differences between classes which give rise to exploitation, the reduction of economic differences between regions and between town and countryside, the provision of full employment, the development of agricultural self-sufficiency, and the integration of agriculture and industry are perhaps the most important five objectives. They are also explicitly or implicitly outlined in SWAPO's Political Programme. For the sake of convenience each will be discussed in turn, although measures to realise them inevitably overlap.

In important respects the first is the pre-condition for the remainder. Nearly all black Namibians are either workers or peasants. Furthermore, the migrant labour system has compelled most peasant households to depend for part of their basic subsistence on wage remittances and approximately half of all black workers and their families spend some or all of their lives in subsistence agriculture. The majority of adult Namibians have therefore experienced rural impoverishment in the reserves and wage exploitation in the towns, mines and ranches as a unified system of oppression.

The demand for structural reform in agriculture is urgent, and the prime focus is likely to be the settler ranches. But peasants living in the bantustans will also expect to see exploitation broken down. The ending of the migrant labour system, which will be a process rather than a sudden change, will be one of the most important objectives. In agriculture itself, expansion of the area of peasant production and improved supporting services are more likely changes than attempts to restructure the way production is organised. The most urgent task will be to replace the present South African-appointed tribal officials, who allocate use-rights over land, by democratic local institutions. In the northern arable areas, the present peasant system is efficient within its limitations, and generally non-exploitative — although women bear a far heavier burden of agricultural labour than men. Under the circumstances, there might be little enthusiasm for an overall change to a collective form of organisation. The special environment also makes thorough trials advisable in the north if any general proposal is made to resettle people into villages from their present dispersed homesteads.

The second objective, reducing inter-regional and rural-urban disparities, is a vital response to the divisions and injustices of apartheid. It also touches one of the most intractable problems of rural development policy, how to achieve an equitable balance in the quality of life between town and country. Where services are provided by the state — education, health, welfare and so on — this is in the first instance a question of general policy on the allocation of scarce resources (skilled personnel even more than finance): how much to spend, on what, and where. Decentralisation of administration and of industry, especially the processing of agricultural products and of goods for local consumption, could also help in the medium term. Perhaps most important will be measures to ensure that peasant households receive an assured and rising income from the sale of their basic products — slaughter sheep and goats and karakul pelts in the south, slaughter cattle and milk in the centre and north, and grain and vegetables in the north. These measures would probably include a strong state initiative in organising the sale and transport of produce — since black Namibians have been largely excluded in the past as middlemen and since the bantustans have been poorly served by existing marketing arrangements.

Government will also be concerned with producer prices for peasant produce, and with prices for goods sold in the rural areas. There are strong arguments for a general policy of subsidies to the rural areas, as part of wider policy on prices and wages, in order to channel development resources from mineral revenues. Subsidies on crop or stock prices have the disadvantage of benefiting most those who sell most — larger producers who may not need most help. Subsidies on inputs — for instance, seed, fertilisers, hoes, small ploughs or means of storage — are more difficult to administer, but can be designed to affect smaller producers more directly, including those who eat rather than sell their crop.

In the achievement of the third objective, full employment, agriculture could potentially play a leading role nationally. The problems, however, are formidable. The colonial suppression of peasant agriculture has left it without the resources for rapid expansion, while over the past 30 years investment in settler ranching has been above all designed to save labour rather than create jobs. Unless early steps are taken to guarantee the cash income of both peasants and farmworkers, a general decline in the rural population is likely. This may have advantages in reducing overcrowding and so raising income for those who remain, but the advantages have to be balanced against the problems of providing work for those who leave. There is little doubt that a reformed ranching sector could support a larger resident population, to some extent of additional single workers but mostly of reunited families of migrant workers. It is possible that a properly organised resettlement programme would succeed, particularly with continuing high urban unemployment, but the colonial experience of contract labour will not attract people to ranches. Furthermore, the integration into the re-organised ranch units of additional settlers, whether from the towns or the reserves, the south or the north, will require careful preparation. Perhaps the greatest long-term prospects of increasing employment are associated with the expansion of arable farming, discussed below.

Closely linked to increased employment is the fourth objective, agricultural self-sufficiency. It raises a complex set of issues and options, most of which cannot be discussed in detail here. Technical and research information is in fact so deficient that one of the most immediate priorities after independence will be to examine whatever records the colonial regime leaves behind, evaluate the advice of remaining ex-colonial experts and foreign consultants, and above all consult widely with peasants and workers on the land. A brief survey of some of the general issues is nevertheless useful.

The key problem at present is the need to import food. This has arisen partly because the ecology of much of Namibia is better suited to pastoral farming, but also because government policy has been biased towards meat and pelts and against both field crops and dairying. An incoming government will want to remove that bias. There are also political and strategic reasons for promoting the cultivation of food crops. In fact, in the long term no substantial decline in pastoral farming would be required, since the population of Namibia is sufficiently small for its cereal and dairy needs to be met from small areas of the country which are relatively well suited to crops.

A start can be made in the short term. The latest FAO estimate is that Namibia will need 310 000 tonnes of cereals a year by 1985,[7] of which only 100 000 tonnes will be grown locally, even in a good year (Appendix Table A5). The FAO study provides a useful discussion of the mechanisms for importing and supplying food, and possibilities for increased production. It is probably true that little can be done in the short term in the north, since the immediately usable arable land is already fully exploited. However, more may be possible in the ranching sector, where some fodder crops are grown at present. The diversion of a proportion of borehole and small dam water within the ranch from stock to the small-scale irrigation of maize and vegetable plots, and a partial switch from fodder to food crops would greatly strengthen food self-sufficiency on the ranches. In the medium term, perhaps the most effective way of increasing arable output, as well as rural employment, would be to encourage closer settlement and increased cultivation in the Otavi highlands, where rainfed field crops give fairly reliable yields and the soil and groundwater are of good quality.

In the long term, substantial increase in crops could be achieved by long-distance transport of water from the northern rivers (Map 5). The necessary investment in dams, canals, pipelines and pumping stations would be very expensive and require searching assessment alongside other development priorities. The skill requirement of irrigation is also notoriously high. The possibilities for increased arable production and employment with such investment are nonetheless considerable. While results would probably be poor on the loose Kalahari sands, intensive irrigation is possible on the good quality soils in parts of the northern hardveld, the terraces of the Okavango valley, and to a limited extent in the Caprivi Strip and parts of the Kaokoveld margin of the sandveld. Irrigation in the Okavango valley, with its salt-free water, gentle gradients, moderately good quality soils and short distances, is probably the most promising and least costly of the prospects. It could possibly be linked with a dam and pumping station towards the northern end of the valley — if the latter proved technically feasible — particularly if associated with pipelines supplying water to other parts of northern Namibia. A dam might also improve the chances of using the alluvial soils of the river

---

7.   FAO 1982, Appendix 2; but see Table A5 and note in this study.

Map 5   Areas of New Agricultural Potential in the North

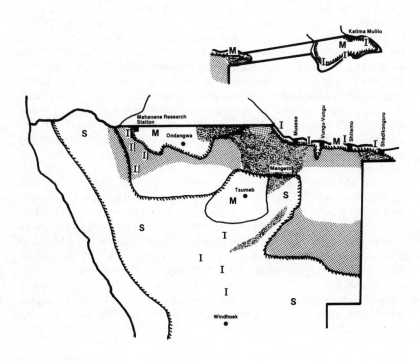

—— International boundaries

⁓⁓⁓ Populated areas (on the hatched side of the line). Except in the extreme north and north-east this settlement is generally very sparse

Areas of new agricultural potential

cattle-raising

mixed stock and arable farming

I localised spray or flood irrigation

Existing farming areas
S   stock farming
M   mixed farming
■   State development schemes

banks, which are flooded each summer, for controlled flood irrigation of such crops as rice and sugar. The same method and crops may also be possible with the drainage and conversion of the swampy river margins of the eastern Caprivi Strip.

Such projects could make Namibia self-sufficient in basic grains, vegetables, fruit, fodder, sugar, oilseeds and cotton, even if the investment costs were not economic in strict accounting terms. Peasant or co-operative organisation might be possible, but this would seem to be a suitable opportunity for implementing the association in SWAPO's Political Programme between state-owned farms, large-scale agricultural production and the commitment to agricultural self-reliance. Together with irrigation from the Orange River and a few smaller-scale irrigation schemes — at the springs of the artesian zones and Kaokoveld, and below the larger dams — this is probably the only means of producing a marketable surplus for the towns, mines and stock-farms.

Another major opportunity for increased production and employment — costing considerably less in operating costs and skills and possibly also in initial investment — would be to open up the belt of land between the Ovambo floodplain and the Okavango River for small-scale settlement. The average rainfall, at above 500mm, is adequate for cereals and so is the soil; already some 60 000 people farm precariously in the area. What is required is a reliable and year-round water supply, to provide not irrigation but drinking water for people and livestock. A network of water-points through the region would expand both the potential area of permanent settlement and the possible density of that settlement: both crops and cattle-raising would yield far more reliable sources of income than at present. The number of small reservoirs and boreholes could probably be substantially increased, but the major supply would be the good quality water of the Okavango River, which is close by. Although the upward gradient would necessitate pumping stations, it is very gradual and the terrain is flat throughout except for low undulating sand-dunes. A settlement scheme such as this, whether organised in villages with attached field and pasturage zones or in the traditional dispersed pattern, offers the one possibility of a major extension of small-scale mixed farming in Namibia.

Although this appears to be the only suitable area for new arable settlement, two other areas offer an opportunity for a significant expansion of stock-raising, if drinking water can be provided for people and animals. In the sandveld south of the Okavango River the density of the bush and tree cover may pose problems for the development of arable farming, but fewer for stock-raising; the same applies to the drier sandveld in the east of the Herero reserve. The second area is the savannah to the south and west of the *oshana* zone, whose carrying capacity may be slightly higher although surface water is less.

Production can therefore be raised by bringing more land into use. Nothing has hitherto been said of productivity: the possibility of increasing production from the existing area of farmland or the existing input of labour. While detailed trials may prove otherwise, it would be unwise to anticipate more than a marginal early increase in productivity from technical innovation in any of the different branches of agriculture.

Such a conclusion may not be surprising in respect of the ranching sector. The birth-rate and offtake of both karakul sheep and beef cattle is probably near its sustainable maximum. The same is broadly true of the far north. Although there is considerable scope for the eradication of endemic diseases and parasites, for improvement of breed, and for increase of the rate of reproduction and offtake, increased efficiency to a certain extent means reduced numbers, because the existing pasture is badly overgrazed, except perhaps in the Caprivi. Above all, a rigorous and comprehensive control on the drilling of boreholes is essential to the proper conservation of grazing and groundwater. Indeed in parts of the ranching zone, upon investigation it may prove advisable to close down some of the existing boreholes as a safety measure. The rapid degeneration of the pasture in the eastern sandveld of Botswana under the pressure of unregulated boreholes is an example to avoid in Namibia. It may likewise be prudent to recover some of the flexibility of the open communal method of pre-colonial range management by planning a network of groups of state-held reserve ranches, to be opened up in case of drought and at other times sparingly used for improving the condition of stock en route to the abattoir.

The difficulty of improving productivity may seem more surprising in arable farming. Nonetheless, the low grain yield in the Ovambo floodplain reflects a very difficult cultivating environment. The dry conditions probably preclude the general replacement of millet by higher-yielding grains like maize; the saline sub-soil makes the use of tractors and deep ploughing risky; and the poverty of the soil may rule out the heavy application of inorganic fertiliser. The traditional techniques of Ovambo field cultivation — planting direct into manured mounds and improving fertility by rotating the homestead and animal kraals within the field area — were well adapted, though they required a large amount of labour and gave low returns on effort expended. Ovambo farmers were therefore reluctant to adopt higher technology methods, although tractor or donkey ploughing is now common. Promotion of such methods after independence would best be preceded by careful trials and through consultation with the farmers themselves. However, the work of ICRISAT (the Institute for Crop Research in Semi-Arid Regions, based in India) in similar environments may provide fruitful examples for Namibian conditions, and experiments with adapting or developing higher yielding and more drought-resistant millet deserve early attention.

Elsewhere in the north the wider use of ploughing, whether animal-drawn or mechanised, may be desirable along with a partial switch from millet to maize. Maize can be grown more reliably and successfully where the rainfall exceeds 550mm per annum (Okavango Valley, Caprivi Strip, Otavi highlands). Fertilisers may be more suitable where the soil is richer (Otavi highlands, northern hardveld). The karstveld (Otavi highlands) has probably the best potential for high grain yields, cattle ranches in the heart of the district recording 11.4 bags per hectare for maize even in the drought year 1969/70. In general, though, intensive methods of land-use, whether pastoral or arable, carry a high degree of risk of poor returns and above all of permanent damage to pasture, soil structure and water reserves in a fragile semi-arid climate such as Namibia's. Careful testing of such methods is highly advisable before introduction on a wide scale. There is perhaps greater potential in the extension of the farm area and in irrigation than in the intensification of existing farming methods, at least in the short term.

The fifth objective, integration of agriculture and industry, concerns first the processing of agricultural produce, both for internal consumption and for export. There is probably scope for expansion in major export commodities: in meat processing and byproduct plant, unless current investment provides enough, and in karakul pelt sorting and possibly also several of the other specialised stages of fur garment manufacture. Wool scouring, weaving, dairy processing, maize and wheat milling, oil pressing (from seeds and nuts), tanning and leather good manufacture, dehydration of vegetables and fruit, all are areas in which existing capacity is either non-existent or inadequate.

Industry is also required for the supply of inputs to agriculture — building materials, machinery, implements, fertilisers, concentrated stockfeed, means of packaging and storage, and engineering and repair services. A SWAPO government, according to its Political Programme, would take a 'keen interest in providing adequate modern tools and instruments for large-scale agricultural production'. In this respect simple tools such as hoes and small motorised or animal-drawn ploughs are more important and more feasible than complex machinery. Small artisan workshops are likely to be cost-effective and more versatile than single large-scale factories, given

Namibia's small demand. In respect of fertilisers and stockfeed it may be noted that Namibia already has important natural resources (guano or bird-dung from the offshore islands, salt from coastal lagoons) and byproducts (fishmeal, bonemeal) which are at present only partially exploited or simply exported.

Finally, it is necessary to return to the first objective, the ending of exploitation, but this time from a different angle, the position of women in the development process. In most discussions of agricultural development in Namibia — Chambers and Green are a partial exception — women receive at best a passing mention. In a sense the same is true of this study, partly because general terms such as 'Namibian', 'worker' and 'peasant' mask basic differences in the roles of male and female members of the same category, partly because the focus has been as much on ecology and resources as on social relationships, and most importantly because of lack of data on women's roles. Nevertheless, as has been pointed out earlier, women have been grievously disadvantaged by the migrant labour system and by open colonial discrimination. Programmes of positive discrimination will be needed to enable them to participate fully in social, economic and political life. SWAPO's Constitution explicitly recognises 'sexism' as a 'reactionary tendency' to be combated by party members in furthering the party's basic aims.

There are at least three basic areas in which systematic action and consciousness-raising are required. First, men need to be reintegrated into the tasks and responsibilities of child-rearing and housework in which they played a substantial, albeit unequal, part in pre-colonial times and from which the long inflexible working hours of farm labour and the splitting of families under migrant labour have all but completely separated them. There is greater flexibility for the sharing of these functions in agriculture, with its variable work-patterns and small-scale organisation, than in the other branches of production.

Second, women need to be given much greater opportunity and training to participate in productive work. In the stock-farming zone this gives added priority to the encouragement of small-scale field and garden cultivation and to irrigation generally, for expansion in this area would create new employment alongside stock-raising. There are also a variety of ancillary jobs in processing, services and transport to which training and an equal opportunity employment policy would give women greater access. The most fundamental change in agriculture as a whole will only come when women are able to work with livestock, particularly cattle. To a degree such a break in the strong traditional exclusion of women has already begun in the northern mixed farming zone in the absence of men away on contract, but it will need systematic reinforcement over a long period to become a general breakthrough. Similarly men need to be encouraged to participate in the central tasks of field cultivation and the collection of wood and water, at present left largely to women; here the use of animal-drawn implements and carts and of irrigation may act as catalysts.

Third, it is vital that women be both consulted and placed in leadership roles in the development process. Too often male administrators communicate only with male heads of households, leading both to the exclusion of women from participation and to inefficiency in the execution of programmes about which men may know little because it is women who undertake the work in question. Bringing women forward into decision-making posts would also strengthen communication and democratic participation. Such a process is already under way within SWAPO; elsewhere there is little sign.

Risks, transition and solidarity

The legacy of German and South African colonialism in Namibian agriculture is a devastating one socially, politically and economically. Its interaction with a fragile environment has been equally disastrous ecologically. The transformation of rural Namibia from extreme exploitation and ecological degradation to an acceptable pattern of rural economy and society will necessarily be both risky and radical. Sheer survival requires that — neither the status quo nor moderate change is viable ecologically or economically any more than socially or politically.

These harsh facts are known by rural Namibians and by the leadership of the liberation movement from their daily experience. It is important that they be recognised also by supporters of the cause of Namibian liberation. The power of entrenched interests in Namibia and of their external allies to resist radical change will not disappear on independence day. The risk of disruption is high in agriculture, whatever South Africa does. If South Africa does seek systematically to disrupt (for example by interference with transport, withdrawal of personnel, closure of markets and obstruction of deliveries, quite apart from the use of military force), dislocation will be that much greater both in agriculture and more generally.

Committed and comprehending solidarity can materially aid in supporting the transition and help the government of Namibia to cope with disruptions and to institute its programmes for rural change. Replacement technical and research personnel, transport support and alternative sources of supply and markets must in the short run be found abroad. Similarly, forward planning based on dialogue can be useful and can be assisted by participation of supporters of Namibian liberation as well as by Namibians. However, it is essential to realise that the prime subjects of rural change in Namibia are and will remain rural Namibians. They have borne the costs of the present system and will bear the brunt of the risks and costs of its transformation. They must take a leading role in determining rural development since only their commitment and awareness, rooted in the long struggle for Namibian liberation, can sustain it.

Statistical Appendix

Table A1

The Place of Agriculture in the Economy

Gross domestic product, 1977 (Million Rand)

PRIMARY SECTOR	Agriculture	Forestry	Fishing	Mining	*Total Primary*
commercial	137.5	1	40	375	553.5
peasant	20 (40)	1 (2)	0.5 (1)	—	21.5 (43)
total	157.5	2	40.5	375	575

SECONDARY SECTOR	Food processing	Other manufacturing	Construction	Utilities	*Total Secondary*
commercial	50	32.5	58	15	155.5
peasant	—	2.5 (5)	2	—	4.5 (7)
total	50	35	60	15	160

TERTIARY SECTOR	Transport, communications, storage	Trade	Accommodation	Finance	Social & personal services	Government	*Total tertiary*	TOTAL GDP (ALL SECTORS)
commercial	57.5	105	22.5	85	50	70	390	1100
peasant	2.5	5	2.5 (10)	—	—	—	10 (17.5)	35 (67.5)
total	60	110	25	85	50	70	400	1135

Notes

Includes Walvis Bay; fish factory production entered under food processing. Peasant output estimated at farm gate prices; brackets indicate the approximate equivalent at retail prices. R1 = £0.66 (1977).

Source

Green 1981, Table 15, with minor amendments.

Table A2

Sales and Exports of Livestock Products, 1961-80

(a) Cattle

	1961	1962	1963	1964	1965	1966	1967	1968	1969	1970
Total sales¹ (000 head)	297	262	361	379	376	300	313	318	312	417
of which: exports — live to SA (%)	78	65	73	68	65	59	77	81	77	75
— processed² (%)	(13)	25	(19)	(25)	28	(32)	(14)	(10)	(14)	(18)
Local fresh meat consumption³ (%)	(9)	10	(8)	(7)	7	(9)	(9)	(9)	(9)	(7)

	1971	1972	1973	1974	1975	1976	1977	1978	1979	1980
Total sales¹ (000 head)	503	583	508	276	326	389	351	397	420	461
of which: exports — live to SA (%)	74	74	64	77	77	67	57	60	54	51
— processed² (%)	(20)	20	30	12	15	24	34	32	39	(42)
Local fresh meat consumption³ (%)	(6)	6	7	11	8	9	10	8	7	(7)

(b) Small stock (sheep and goats)

	1961	1962	1963	1964	1965	1966	1967	1968
Total sales (000 head)	147	142	180	234	193	203	327	399
of which: live exports to SA (%)	59	48	57	65	56	51	68	72

	1978	1979	1980
Total sales (000 head)	370	369	336
Live exports to SA (%)	68	67	61

(c) Karakul pelts

	1961	1962	1963	1964	1965	1966	1967	1968	1969	1970
Total sales (000 pelts)	2022	2346	2274	2864	2241	2977	2896	3421	3642	3347

	1971	1972	1973	1974	1975	1976	1977	1978	1979	1980
Total sales (000 pelts)	3429	3416	3180	2954	2985	2818	2611	2710	2899	2707

Notes

1. Including peasant sales.
2. Total sales less live exports + local consumption. Only a small proportion of canned beef output is marketed locally.
3. Figures in brackets are derived from projected estimates of local consumption.

Sources

Kontak Aug. 1980, p.2, Table 1; *Namibia/SWA Prospectus*, Table 1; *SWA Survey 1967*, p.64; *Windhoek Advertiser*, 18 Dec. 1981; Schneider 1977, Tables 3-5, 8; SWA Karakul Board, *Annual Report 1978/9*.

Table A3

Various Official Estimates of Value of Agricultural Production, 1975-80[1]

(a) At Current Prices   *Rands million*

Source		1975	1976	1977	1978	1979	1980	1981
A.	Beef	54.7	63.0	58.7	67.7			
	Karakul pelts	33.4	46.4	37.1	31.1			
	Mutton	10.8	11.3	12.0	11.7			
	Wool	1.8	2.6	2.9	3.2			
	Other	11.2	13.3	15.0	16.5			
	Total output	*112*	*137*	*126*	*130*			
B.	Beef	54.7	63.0	55.2	62.7	77.6		
	Karakul pelts	33.4	46.4	37.1	31.1	45.1		
	Mutton	10.3	10.5	10.4	10.4	12.7		
	Wool	1.8	2.6	2.9	3.2	2.3		
	Other	11.2	13.3	14.9	16.1	17.2		
	Total	*111*	*136*	*120*	*124*	*155*		
C.	*Total*	*101*	*122*	*107*	*101*	*109*	*(116)* [2]	
D.	*Total*	*112*	*131*	*115*	*113*	*116*		
E.	*Total agriculture and fishing*	*112*	*132*	*112*	*105*	*111*	*128*	
	Gross value added in agriculture						98	(115) (165)[2,3]

Notes
1. All sources except possibly sources D and E exclude non-marketed production, and hence most peasant output.
2. Fourth quarter projected from first three on previous year's pattern.
3. This increase over 1980 due to widespread selling of livestock herds due to drought: in the long term this will reduce production.

Sources
A — *Namibia/SWA Prospectus 1980*, Table 6: 'Gross Value of Agricultural Production'.
B — Leistner 1981, Table 6: 'Gross Value of Agricultural Production'.
C — *Economic Statistics* No.1, 1980, Table 1: 'Agriculture: Gross Domestic Product at Factor Costs' (may also include forestry).
D — *On the Economic Front*, No.3, 1980, pp.2-3: 'Gross Domestic Product at Current Prices: Agriculture, Forestry and Fishing' (excluding Walvis Bay).
E — *Statistical/Economic Review 1982*, p.21: 'Gross Domestic Product at Current Prices, Agriculture and Fishing' and p.39: 'Gross Value Added in Agriculture'.

(b) Index of Value of Agricultural Output in Constant Prices[1]

Index (1975 = 100)

Source		1975	1976	1977	1978	1979	1980
A.		100	102	83	76		
B.		100	102	80	73	79	
C.		100	101	78	65	61	
D.		100	98	76	66	59	
E.	(includes fishing)	100	103	87	75	71	70

Notes
1. Current price totals from above table, deflated by the South African farm
requisites cost index (year to June) as follows:

1975	1976	1977	1978	1979
100	120	135	153	176

Except Source E, which prints its own table at constant prices (p.20).

Table A4
Patterns of Land-use, 1982

(million hectares)

Land Use Zone[1]	Sector Commercial	Peasant	Total
Hardveld: mixed arable and stock	1.4	—	1.4
stock-raising: large	7.1	0.6[2]	7.7
transitional	6.0	2.1[2]	8.1
small	13.5	7.8	21.3
total hardveld	*28.0*	*10.5*	*38.5*
Sandveld: mixed arable + stock	1.35	2.65	4.0
stock-raising: large	1.5	2.4	3.9
transitional	1.8	0.3	2.1
small	3.35	0.15	3.5
total sandveld	*8.0*	*5.5*	*13.5*
Total Farm Land: mixed arable + stock	2.75	2.65	5.4
stock-raising: large	8.6	3.0	11.6
transitional	7.8	2.4	10.2
small	16.85	7.95	24.8
Total (hardveld and sandveld)	*36.0[1]*	*16.0*	*52.0*
Barren	0.6	17.4	18.0
Total distribution between sectors	*36.6*	*33.4[3]*	*70.0*

Notes
1. See map 3 and text p.11 for definition of land use zones.
2. About half (1.5m ha) is mountainous terrain in the Kaokoveld.
3. These values calculated from official data; all others are estimated & hence
approximate. The land-use categories reflect existing technology & investment.

Sources
Estimated from maps and land-use data.

Table A5

(a) Food Balance: Cereal Production and Requirements, Early 1970s

	Peasant areas			Total Peasant Arable	Stock-raising Reserves	White farms and towns	Total
	Ovamboland	Okavango	East Caprivi				
Production (000 tonnes)	40	8	3	51	1	23	75
Needs (000 tonnes)	53	9.5	4.5	67	12	66	145
Deficit (000 tonnes)	13	1.5	1.5	16	11	43	70
Deficit as % of Needs (%)	25	16	33	24	92	65	48

The estimates given here depend on a series of assumptions. Figures for grain output and resident population are taken from official sources, whose tendency to understate is roughly similar. The harvest is assumed to be good but not exceptional (when it could be up to 50% higher). The total for Ovamboland includes 35 000 tonnes of millet and 5 000 of sorghum. Reported figures of 4 600 tonnes for the Okavango valley (1970/1) and 1 300 tonnes for the eastern Caprivi Strip appear too low — as do rates of yield — and have been increased here. In the commercial sector, official estimates for the maize crop of 12-15 000 tonnes *(Namibia/SWA Prospectus 1980, Agricultural Census 1970/71)* and 9 000-10 000 tonnes (SWA Grain Board) seem grossly to underestimate small-scale cultivation on ranches, which one survey (Carstens 1971) implies could push the total over 30 000 tonnes. Since such cultivation risks high losses in the sub-marginal climate and since a proportion may be used unripe as fodder, the total has been reduced to 20 000 tonnes. Official estimates of wheat output are likewise too low at 250-300 tonnes (SWA Grain Board) and have been increased to 3 000 tonnes, most of it grown at the Hardap Dam irrigation scheme. Human cereal requirements are assessed here at the level of minimum needs, given in a recent FAO report (FAO 1982) as an average 450g a day per person. If a 10% loss is attributed to storage, handling and transport, annual requirements average 180kg (2 bags) per person. It should be noted that by the early 1980s actual needs and the grain deficit were undoubtedly greater than stated here, owing to drought, war and aggravated underdevelopment.

Sources

SWA Grain Board, *Annual Reports; SWA Survey 1967*, Table 7; *Agricultural Census 1970/1*, Table 3.1; *Namibia/SWA Prospectus 1980*, Table 6; Stellenbosch 1978, p.43; Stellenbosch 1980, Tables 86-87; Nixon 1978, p.7; press reports.

Table A5

(b) Food Balance: FAO Estimate of Production and Requirements, 1985[1]

(tonnes)	Ovamboland	Okavango	Eastern Caprivi Strip	Total	Rest of Namibia	Whole Country
Grain requirement	122 450	22 320	9 420[2]	154 190	155 810	310 000
Local production				70 000	30 000	100 000
Import needs				84 190	125 810	210 000

Notes

1. These statistics given in the recent FAO report appear not wholly plausible. South African estimates of normal millet production in Ovamboland of 30 000-35 000 tonnes (p.2.8), and in the whole of the far north of 25 000-42 000 tonnes (p.2.28) are tentatively supported, which together with 8 000-12 000 tonnes of maize (p.2.28) give a combined total of 33 000-54 000 tonnes plus an unstated but small quantity of sorghum and wheat. Later, however, total grain output in the far north is put at 60 000-70 000 tonnes, marketed maize at 15 000-20 000 tonnes, and national grain production in normal years at 100 000 tonnes (p.3.3). As the basis of calculation of the second set of figures is not stated, this large inconsistency remains unexplained. Even allowing for population increase, the estimates of grain requirements (Appendix 2), which are based on a theoretical minimum need for daily consumption per person and a population projected from UNIN estimates, seem too high given probable current levels of grain imports: either population is overstated, or grain output understated, or there is mass malnutrition. The figures appear most improbable in the case of Ovamboland: the gap between 1985 annual needs (122 500 tonnes) and 'normal' grain output (35 000 tonnes) implies that over 70% (87 500 tonnes) of the cereal requirement must be imported. With current levels of imports at some 20 000 tonnes the grain actually available would be at present no more than about half what the resident population needs for survival without malnutrition. In practice, South African statistics for population and grain output are probably both somewhat understated, but not to the extent suggested by the FAO. Although any estimate is bound to be speculative, the national grain requirement, using the FAO's criteria, may well reach around 250 000 tonnes by 1985, with a deficit of 175 000 tonnes (145 000 tonnes actually consumed) to be met by imports.

2. The figure given in Appendix 2 (540 tonnes) is clearly an error. Subtraction down the column gives 18 910 tonnes, along the row 9 420 tonnes, which is probably the figure intended.

Source
FAO 1982.

Table A6

Estimate of Peasant Sales and Income from Stock 1979

Bantustan	Namaland[a]				Kaokoland[b]			Damaraland		Rehoboth		
	Cattle	Small stock	Karakul pelts	Total	Cattle	Small stock	Total	Cattle	Total	Cattle	Karakul pelts	Total
Sales: no (000)	0.63	9.8	54		3	1		9[c]		4	130	
value[d] (R000)	56	107	604	767	357	13	370	1100		480	1700	2180
offtake[j] (%)	8	7	37		3			15		10	65[e]	
Per household[f]: no	*0.16*	*2.6*	*14*		*0.73*	*0.24*		*2.3*		*1.5*	*58*	
value (R)	*15*	*28*	*159*	*202*	*87*	*3*	*90*	*290*		*185*	*655*	*840*

Bantustan	Hereroland	Ovambo				Kavango	Whole country[g]			
	Cattle	Cattle	Small stock	Pigs	Total	Cattle	Cattle	Small stock	Karakul pelts	Total
Sales: no (000)	47[c]	8	6[h]	1[h]		2	74	17	184	
value (R000)	5640	800	60	40	900	200[i]	8635	215	2300	11 150
offtake (%)	16	1.5	1.5		–	2.5	54	1.40		
Per household: no	*6.5*	*0.07*	*0.05*	*0.01*		*1.1*				
value (R)	*780*	*7.15*	*0.50*	*0.35*	*8*	*11*				*14.60*

Notes

a. Year to March 1979, compared with which in the year 1979 pelt prices were up 25% and slaughter stock prices up 15%.
b. Assuming a rough doubling of sales in 1975/6, the last available figures (cattle 1739 head, small stock 416).
c. Assuming an almost equal rate of offtake for the combined total of 56 000 cattle sold in Hereroland and Kaokoland in 1979.
d. In 'Namaland' cattle averaged R90 per head in 1978/9. Assumed mean prices for 1979 elsewhere were R120 per head, but R100 for the smaller Ovambo and Kavango animals. Likewise, small stock prices were R11, R13 and R10 per head respectively. Settler cattle averaged R185 in 1979 and mutton R32 per head in 1978.
e. An assumed rate, from which the volume of sales is derived. The ranch offtake for 1979 was 90%.
f. Numbers of households taken from Table 1.
g. Almost complete in respect of cattle, less so for small stock and pelts. No estimates at all are available for dairy products, hides and skins.
h. The 1973/4 level plus 50%.
i. 1975/6 prices plus 50%.
j. Offtake is here defined as the ratio of beasts sold per annum to total herd size.

Sources

Department of Coloured Relations, *Annual Report 1978/9; Kontak* April 1980, pp.3, 10-11; Stellenbosch 1978, Tables 6.1, 6.4; Stellenbosch 1980, Table 83-4; Stellenbosch 1976, Tables 11 and 13.

Table A7

Various Estimates of Average Income and Expenditure per Farm on Settler Ranches (Rand)

Group	1	2	3	4[a]	5[a]	6	7
Type of farm	cattle	all	all	all	cattle	karakul	cattle
Year	1969/70	1970/1	1977/8	1977/8	1977/8	1977/8	1977/8
Gross income	16 693	14 000[b]	32 000[b]	35 000	15 500	41 252	35 369
Costs: recurrent: wages[c]	1 913	1 673	3 712			3 107	4 241
other	2 544[d]	4 922	4 885[d]			7 779	13 505
total	4 457	6 595	8 597			10 886	17 746
capital: fixed	1 301[d]	1 387	2 931[d]				
moveable	2 057[d]	1 594	3 908[d]				
total	3 358	2 981	6 839			3 794[e]	3 063[e]
Debt servicing[f]: mortgages	1 227	1 110					
other	(501)[g]	445					
total	1 728	1 553	1 954			(3 000)[h]	(3 200)[h]
Total Costs	*9 543*	*11 129*	*17 390*	*18 000*	*12 000*	*16 480*	*24 009*
Net income	7 150	2 871	14 610	17 000	3 500	24 512	11 360
Proportion of turnover (%)	43	21	46	49	23	60	32

Farm Groups

1. Sample of northern cattle ranches (Tsumeb, Grootfontein, Otjiwarongo districts).
2-3. All farms.
4. Top 20% profit-earning ranches out of unspecified number.
5. Ranches in the Tsumeb district in the 50-60% profit band.
6. Average of 15 account-keeping karakul ranches.
7. Average of 24 account-keeping cattle ranches.

Notes

a. Assuming a ranch size of 6 000 hectares.
b. Assuming 5 118 farms and excluding peasant sales.
c. Either wages (groups 2 + 3) or total labour costs (group 1, probably also 6 + 7).
d. In respect of fixed improvements and implements, recurrent and capital items are not distinguished. Here they have been included under capital expenditure.
e. Depreciation only. (Fixed improvements 4%, moveables 20%), and therefore probably understated.
f. Calculated at 10% (capital and interest) of the amount owed.
g. Calculated at the 1970/1 ratio of 29% of total debts.
h. Taking outstanding Land Bank mortgages at their 1970/1 ratio of 41% of total farm debts and correcting for the differing average land values between the two groups.

Sources

Carstens 1971, Tables 12-14; *Agricultural Census 1970/1*, Tables 1.1, 2.2-3, 4.3-5, 5.1-3, 7.1; Green 1981, Tables 5, 8, 22; Nixon 1978, p.3-4; Brandt 1979, Table 4.

Table A8

Estimated Productivity and Profitability on Settler Ranches

Group[a] Type of farm Year	(Unit)	Average per farm		4 ?All 1977/8	5 Cattle 1977/8	6 Karakul 1977/8	7 Cattle 1977/8
		1 Cattle 1969/70	2 All 1970/1				
Area	ha	6 305	7 250			10 753	7 658
Livestock	LSU[b]	633	(535)			489	629
Capital[c]	R	147 800	148 000			217 000	318 000
Income[d]: gross	R	16 693	14 000			41 252	35 369
net	R	7 150	2 871			24 512	11 360
Return on capital: gross	%	11.3	9.5	16.5	10.0	19.0	11.1
net	%	4.8	1.9	8.1	2.2	11.3	3.6
Income per LSU[d]: gross	R	26.37	26.17			84.36	56.23
net	R	11.30	5.37			50.13	18.06
Income per ha: gross	R	2.63	1.93	5.84	2.58	3.84	4.62
net	R	1.13	0.40	2.86	0.56	2.28	1.48
Capital per ha	R	23.44	20.41			20.18	41.52

Notes

a. See Table A7.

b. One livestock unit = 1 head of cattle (over 2 years)/mule/donkey/horse = 2 head of cattle (0-2 years) = 6 sheep/goats = 5 pigs = 100 poultry. In the case of group 2, for which complete figures are not available, the stated average is within 10% of official estimates either way.

c. Land, fixed and moveable improvements, and livestock. The stated valuation for group 2, which is taken to cover land and fixed improvements only, has been increased by the appropriate ratio for 1969/70 (59% of total assets).

d. Includes income from non-livestock sources (c. 3% of gross sales). Excludes gains in weight and retained offtake of livestock. Losses during the drought year 1977/8 would therefore overstate income here.

Sources

Table A7 and references cited therein.

Bibliography

Books and articles

Africa Institute (SA), *Namibia/SWA Prospectus*, (Pretoria, 1980).

Albertyn, G.B., 'Produksiekoste van karakoelpelse vir ses plase in Sinclairomgewing vir 1969/70 en 1970/71', *KBSSA Yearbook*, 14, 1971/72.

Anschel, K.R., & Brannon, R.H., *The Agricultural Sector of Namibia: a Brief Assessment*, (US Dept of Agriculture, staff paper, 1978).

Anti-Apartheid Movement et al., *Namibian Karakul: an International Slave Trade*, (London, 1972).

Asombang, W.W., 'Export marketing strategies for economic development', SADEX, 11-12/80.

Bähr, J., *Kulturgeographische Wandlungen in der Farmzone SWAs*, (*Bonner Geographische Abhandlungen*, 40, 1968).

Bähr, J., 'Strukturwandel der Farmwirtschaft in SWA', *Zeitschrift für ausländische Wirtschaft*, 9(2), 1970.

Banghart, P.D., 'The effects of the migrant labourer on the Ovambo of SWA', *Fort Hare Papers*, 5(4), 1972.

Bley, H., *SWA under German rule, 1894-1914*, (Heinemann, London, 1971).

Borchert, G., *Südostangola: Landschaft, Landschafthaushalt und Entwicklungsmöglichkeiten im Vergleich zum zentralen Hochland von Mittelangola*, (*Hamburger Geographische Studien*, 17, 1963).

Brandt, H., *Sektorstudie Landwirtschaft*, (German Development Institute, Berlin, 1979). Short version in English in GDI 1980.

Bruwer, J.P., *SWA: the disputed land*, (Nasionale Boekhandel, Cape Town, 1966).

Carstens, N.W., *An Economic Analysis of Farming in the Northern Beef Cattle Areas of SWA, 1970*, (SA, Dept of Agricultural Economics and Marketing, Pretoria, 1971).

Carvalho, E.C., '"Traditional" and "modern" patterns of cattle raising in south-western Angola: a critical evaluation of change from pastoralism to ranching', *Journal of Developing Areas*, 1974.

CIIR/British Council of Churches, *Namibia in the 1980s*, (London, 1981).

Chambers, R. & Green, R.H., 'Agrarian change', in Green 1981.
Chicago Committee for African Liberation, *This is the Time:* interview with two Namibian women, (1977).
Cronje, G. & S., *The Workers of Namibia*, (International Defence and Aid Fund, London, 1979).
Dentlinger, U., *An Ethnobotanical Study of the !Nara Plant among the Topnaar Hottentots of Namibia*, (Munger Africana Library Notes, 38, 1977).
Drechsler, H., *Let us Die Fighting: the Struggle of the Herero and Nama against German Imperialism, 1884-1915*, (Zed Press, London, 1980).
Du Pisani, E., 'Some aspects of animal husbandry in Kavango', *Namib und Meer*, 8, 1978.
Eggers, H., 'Das Ovamboland', *Geog. Rundschau*, 18, 1966.
FAO, Namibia Nationhood Programme, *Sectoral Planning Workshop on Agriculture, Fisheries and Food Security: Papers and Reports of Working Groups*, (Maputo, 1980).
FAO, Namibia Nationhood Programme, *Food Supplies and Nutrition in Namibia*, (FAO/Overseas Development Group, University of East Anglia, 1982, draft report).
FAO, *Namibia: Prospects for Future Development*, (draft report, Rome, 1977).
Financial Mail, 'SWA: special surveys', (20 Aug. 1965 and 2 Mar. 1973).
First, R., *South West Africa*, (Penguin, Harmondsworth, 1963).
First, R. & Segal, R., *SWA: Travesty of Trust*, (Deutsch, London, 1967).
Fraenkel, P., *The Namibians of South West Africa*, (Minority Rights Group, London, 1978).
Gad, J., *Die Betriebsverhältnisse der Farmen des mittleren Hererolandes*, (Hamburg, 1915).
Gebhardt, F.B., 'The socio-economic status of farm labourers in Namibia', in *SA Labour Bulletin* 1978.
Gellert, J.F., 'Klimabedingtheit und wirtschaftsgeographische Struktur der Farmwirtschaft in SWA', *Erdkunde*, 2, 1949.
German Development Institute, *Perspectives of independent development in southern Africa: the cases of Zimbabwe and Namibia*, (Berlin, 1980).
Giess, W., 'A preliminary vegetation map of SWA', *Dinteria*, 4, (Nov. 1971).
Gordon, R., 'Variations in migration rates: the Ovambo case', *Journal of Southern African Affairs*, 3(3), 1978.
Green, L.G., *Lords of the Last Frontier*, (Timmins, Cape Town, 1952).
Green, R.H., *Namibia: a Political Economic Survey*, (discussion paper, Institute of Development Studies, Sussex, 1979).
Green, R.H., *From Südwestafrika to Namibia: the Political Economy of Transition*, (research report 58, Scandinavian Institute of African Studies, 1981).
Green, R.H., Kiljunen M-L., & Kiljunen, K., *Namibia: the Last Colony*, (Longman, London, 1981).
Gundry, H., 'Some features of war-time finance and exchange control in the SWA karakul trade', *SA Journal of Economics*, 13, 1945.
Halbach, A.J., 'SWA: Klima, Wasserhaushalt und landwirtschaftliche

Nutzung eines semiariden Trockenraumes', *Jahrbuch der Wittheit zu Bremen*, 10, 1966.

Halbach, A.J., 'Landwirtschaftliche Nutzungsmöglichkeiten eines semiariden Trockenraumes', *Jahrbuch der Wittheit zu Bremen*, 11, 1967.

Hansen, C.P.A., 'The agricultural economy of SWA', *Agrekon*, 5(4), 1966.

Herrigel, O., 'Namibian agriculture: the challenge ahead', paper, Ditchley Park Conference, 1981.

Hüsser, K., 'Der Niederschlagsgang und die Niederschlagsverteilung im Gebiet des Erongo mittleres SWA', *SWASS Journal*, 30, 1975/6.

Jenkins, T. & Brain, C.K., *The peoples of the lower Kuiseb valley, SWA*, Namib Desert Research Station, scientific papers, 35, 1967.

Jenny, H., *Südwestafrika* (Kohlhammer Verlag, Stuttgart/Berlin, 1966).

Joubert, J.G.V. & van der Westhuizen, F.G.J., 'Die invloed van verskillende veedigthede teen dieselfde veebeladings op die produksie van jong groeiende ossies op oshona grasveld', *Proceedings of the Grassland Society of SA*, 15, 1980.

Joubert, J.G.V., *Weidingsbeheer in Suid- en Suidwesafrika*, (Universiteits Uitgewers en Boekhandelaars, Grahamstown, 1974).

Kirsten, G.J.C., 'The production and marketing of karakul pelts', *Agrekon*, 5(3), 1966.

Krogh, D.C., 'Economic aspects of the karakul industry', *SA Journal of Economics*, 23(2), 1955.

Larson, T.J., 'The ethnic composition and environmental influences upon the lower Okavango River population of SWA and Botswana', paper, African Studies Association (US), annual meeting, 1973.

Lee, R.B., 'Mongongo: ethnography of a major wild food resource', *Ecology of Food and Nutrition*, 2, 1971/3.

Lee, R.B., *The !Kung San: Men, Women and Work in a Foraging Society*, (Cambridge University Press, 1979).

Lee, R.B. & Devore, I. (eds), *Kalahari Hunter-Gatherers: Studies of the !Kung San and their Neighbours*, (Harvard University Press, Cambridge, Mass., 1976).

Lehmann, F.R., 'Die anthropogeographische Verhältnisse des Ambolandes im nördlichen SWA', *Zeitschrift für Ethnologie*, 79, 1954.

Lempp, F. (ed.), *Water affairs in SWA*, (Afrika-Verlag der Kreis, Windhoek, 1963).

Leistner, G.M.E., 'SWA/Namibia's economic problems viewed in Africa context', *Bulletin of the Africa Institute of South Africa*, Vol.21 No.11 & 12, 1981.

Lensing, J.E. & Joubert, E., 'Intensity distribution patterns for five species of problem animals in SWA', *Madoqua*, 10(2), 1976.

Le Roux, P.J., 'Bestuur en produksie by die karakoel', *KBSSA Yearbook*, 1978.

Leser, H., *Landschaftsökologische Studien im Kalaharisandgebiet um Auob und Nossob*, (F. Steiner, Wiesbaden, 1971).

Leser, H., 'Landschaftsökologische Grundlageforschung in Trockengebieten: dargestellt an Beispielen aus der Kalahari und ihren Randlandschaften', *Erdkunde*, 25, 1971.

Leser, H., 'Weidewirtschaft und Regenfeldbau im Sandfeld: westliche Kalahari um Schwarzen Nossob und Epukiro, östliches SWA', *Geog. Rundschau*, 27, 1975.

Louw, W., 'Mangetti, home of cattle and knowledge', *SWA Annual* 1980.

Magura, W., *Die Entwicklung der Landwirtschaft in den Bantugebieten von Süd-und Südwestafrika*, (IFO-Institut für Wirtschaftsforschung, Munich, 1970).

Malan, J.S., *The Peoples of SWA/Namibia*, (HAUM, Pretoria, 1980).

Melber, H., *Schule und Kolonialismus: das formale Erziehungswesen Namibias*, (Institut für Afrika-Kunde, Hamburg, 1979).

Moorsom, R.J.B. & Clarence-Smith, W.G., 'Underdevelopment and class-formation in Ovamboland, 1845-1915', *Journal of African History*, 16(3), 1975.

Moorsom, R.J.B., 'Underdevelopment and class-formation: the birth of the contract labour system in Namibia, 1900-26', *York University, Centre for Southern African Studies, Collected Seminar Papers*, 5, 1978/9.

Moorsom, R.J.B., 'Underdevelopment, contract labour and worker consciousness in Namibia, 1915-72', *Journal of Southern African Studies*, 4(1), 1977.

Nixon, C.J., *Land use and development in Namibia*, report, UNIN, Division of Agriculture and Land Resources, 1978.

Ölhafen von Schöllenbach, H., *Die Besiedlung Deutsch-Südwestafrikas bis zum Weltkriege*, (Berlin, 1926).

Opperman, D.J.P., *Algemene oorsig van weidingtoestande in Owambo*, (Windhoek, undated).

Schneider-Barthold, W., *Namibia's Dependency in External Economic Affairs: Options for Reorientation*, in GDI 1980.

Seely, M.K., 'Grassland productivity: the desert end of the curve', *SA Journal of Science*, 74, 1978.

Soini, S., 'Agriculture in northern Namibia: Owambo and Kavango, 1965-70', *Journal of the Scientific Agricultural Society of Finland*, 53, 1981.

SA Labour Bulletin, *Focus on Namibia*, 4(1-2), 1978.

SWAPO of Namibia, Dept. of Information and Publicity, *To Be Born a Nation: the Liberation Struggle for Namibia*, (Zed Press, London, 1981).

SWAPO of Namibia, Central Committee, *Constitution, Political Programme*, (both Lusaka, 1976).

SWA Scientific Society, *Die ethnischen Gruppen in SWA*, (Windhoek, 1965).

Stals, E.L.P., 'Die geskiedenis van die beesteelt in SWA tydens die duitse tydperk, 1884-1915', *Archives Yearbook for SA History*, 1962.

Stellenbosch University (Claassen, P.E. & Page, D.), *Ontwikkelingsplan vir Owambo*, (Institute for Planning Research, 1978).

Stellenbosch University (Page, D., ed.), *'n Raamwerk vir Ontwikkeling van Kavango*, (Institute for Planning Research, 1980).

Stellenbosch University (Page, D., ed.), *Kaokoland: evaluasie van hulpbronne en ontwikkelingsvoorstelle* (Institute for Planning Research, 1976).

Stengel, H.W., 'Die wasserwirtschaftliche Entwicklung einer Farm in SWA', *SWASS Journal*, 17, 1962/3.

Stengel, H.W., *The Black Nosob*, (SWASS, Windhoek, 1966).

Stengel, H.W., *Wasserspeicherung in den Sanden eines Riviers*, (SWASS, Windhoek, 1968).

Thomas, W.H., *Economic Development in Namibia*, (Kaiser/Grünewald, Munich, 1978).

Troup, F., *In Face of Fear*, (London, 1950).

UN Institute for Namibia (Green, R.H.), *Manpower Estimates and Development Implications for Namibia*, (Lusaka, 1978).

UN Institute for Namibia (Mshonga, S.), *Toward Agrarian Reform: Policy Options for Namibia*, (Lusaka, 1979).

UN Institute for Namibia (Asombang, W.W.), *Trade Policy Options for Independent Namibia*, (working paper, Economics Division, Lusaka, 1982).

Urquhart, A., *Patterns of Settlement and Subsistence in Southwestern Angola*, (Washington, 1963).

Van der Waal, B.C.W., 'Namibia: exploitation of fish in Caprivi and Owambo', in: Hobson, G., *A Survey of Fish Farming in Southern Africa*, (University of Cape Town, SALDRU, working paper 18, 1978).

Van Niekerk, J.P. & Bester, F.V., 'Doeltreffende veldbenutting an veldbestuur vir optimale produksie', *KBSSA Yearbook 1978*.

Volk, O.H., *Die Gräser des Farmgebietes von SWA*, (SWASS, Windhoek, 1974).

Von Marees, H.J., 'Die karakoelbedryf: 'n kritiese ekonomiese beskouing', *KBSSA Yearbook 1977*.

Wagner, G., 'Aspects of conservatism and adaptation in the economic life of the Herero', *Sociologus* N.F., 2(1), 1952.

Walter, H. & Volk, O.H., *Grundlagen der Weidewirtschaft in SWA*, (Eugen Ulmer Verlag, Stuttgart, 1954).

Wellington, J.H., *SWA and its Human Issues*, (Clarendon Press, Oxford, 1967).

Wilcox, D.G., 'Aspects of veld management in SA and SWA', typescript report on field visit, 1976.

Wilken, J.J.J. & Fox, G.J., *The History of the Port and Settlement of Walvis Bay 1968-1978*, Johannesburg, 1978.

Theses and dissertations

Banghart, P.D., 'Migrant labour in SWA and its effects on Ovambo tribal life', (MA, Stellenbosch, 1969).

Barnard, W.S., 'Die streekpatrone van SWA', (PhD, Stellenbosch, 1964).

Bruwer, J.P., 'The Kwanyama of SWA', (typescript, Stellenbosch, 1962).

Gebhardt, F.B., 'Der soziale und ökonomische Status der Farmarbeiter in Namibia', (MA, Frankfurt, 1975).

Hanssen, C.P.A., 'Agro-ekonomiese vergelyking tussen drie beesweisstreke in SWA', (MSc, Pretoria, 1967).

Hurlich, S., 'Reserves, migrant labour and the karakul industry in Namibia: a historical perspective', (typescript draft, Toronto, 1982).

Mbamba, A.M., 'Possibilities for the future development of livestock ranching in an independent Namibia', (MPhil, Sussex, 1977).

Moorsom, R.J.B., 'The political economy of Namibia to 1945', (MA, Sussex, 1973).
Olivier, M.J., 'Inboorlingbeleid en -administrasie in die mandaatgebied van SWA', (PhD, Stellenbosch, 1961).
Nixon, C.D., 'Land use and development in Namibia', (MDevtStud, Institute of Social Studies, Hague, 1980).
Schneider, H., 'Analyse der Tiergesundheitssituation in SWA/Namibia: Vergangenheit und Gegenwart', (PhD, Justus-Liebig-Universität, Giessen, 1977).
Van Tonder, L.L., 'The Hambukushu of Okavangoland', (MA, Port Elizabeth, 1966).

Newspapers, journals and yearbooks

CT: *Cape Times.*
RDM: *Rand Daily Mail.*
WA: *Windhoek Advertiser.*
WO: *Windhoek Observer.*
First National Development Corporation (FNDC/ENOK): *Kontak* (approx. monthly).
Namibia Dawn Promotions: *Spectrum* (approx. bimonthly).
SA, Dept. of Agriculture: *Agrekon* (quarterly).
SWA/Namibia, Dept. of Finance: *Economic Statistics* (irreg.); *On the Economic Front* (irreg.).
Karakulbreeders' Association of SWA/SA: *Yearbook* (merged with SA equivalent in 1970).
McGregor, R.: *McGregor's Who Owns Whom*, (Purdey Publishing Co., Somerset West, SA, irreg.).
Meat Producers' Association (SWA): *Annual Report.*
Southwest Agency Co.: *SWA Handbook.*
SWA Agricultural Union: *Annual Report.*
SWA/Namibia, Dept of Finance: *Statistical/Economic Review* (1981-).
SWA Publications: *SWA Annual.*
SWASS (SWA Scientific Society): *Journal* (annual).

Government publications

(a) Annual Reports

SA, Bantu Investment Corporation.
SA, Ekuliko Kavango Ltd (only 1976/7 to date).
SA, Owambo Development Corporation (only 1976/7 to date).
SA, Dept of Agricultural Economics and Marketing.
SA, Dept of Bantu Administration and Development.
SA, Dept of Coloured Relations.
SA, Dept of Finance, *SWA account, estimates of revenue and expenditure.*
SWA Admin., *White paper on the activities of the different branches.*

SWA Admin., Dept of Agricultural Credit and Land Tenure.
SWA Admin., Dept of Agricultural Technical Services.
SWA Admin., Water Affairs Branch (transferred to SA, Dept of Water Affairs).
SWA Administrator (1917-46).
SWA Dairy Industry Control Board.
SWA Grain Board.
SWA Karakul Board (merged 1969-79 with SA Karakul Board).
SWA Land and Agricultural Bank (merged 1969-79 with SA Land Bank).
SWA Meat Trade Control Board.
SWA Promotion of Farming Interests Board.

(b) Other Reports

SA, *Commission of Enquiry into SWA Affairs* (Odendaal), (RP12-64).
SA, Weather Bureau *Drought Investigation Commission of SWA,* (WB600/5/49).
SA, *Commission of enquiry into Alleged Irregularities Relating to the Meat Trade Industry in SWA*, (RP56-80).
SA, National Marketing Council, *Investigation into the marketing of agricultural products in SWA*, (descriptive title only, see SWA Grain Board, *Annual Report* 1972).
SWA Admin., *Native Reserves Commission* (1922).
SWA Admin., *Drought Investigation Commission* (1924).
SWA Legislative Assembly, *Committee on Native Reserves* (LA2-28).
SWA Admin., *Minimum Area of Farms Commission* (1946).
SWA Admin., *Native Labourers Commission* (1948).
SWA Admin., *Long-term Agricultural Policy Commission* (1949).
SA, Dept of Statistics, *Population Census*, 1921, 1960, 1970.
SA, Dept of Agriculture, *Agricultural Census*, 1970/1.
SA, Dept of Water Affairs, SWA Branch, Several regional and national water plans (unpublished).
SA, Dept of Water Affairs, SWA Branch, Report on soil conditions, (Hunting, Loxton and Associates, unpublished).
SA, Dept of Bantu Admin. and Development, *Five-year Plan for the Development of the Native Areas*, (?1967).
SA, Dept of Bantu Admin. and Development, *Verslag van die interdepartementele Komitee insake waterbenutting en algemene landbouonttwikkeling in die Oostelike Caprivistrook*, (Pretoria, 1969, unpublished).
FNDC/ENOK, Regional surveys of investment opportunities (completed by 1981: Namaland, Damaraland, Rehoboth Gebiet, all unpublished).
FNDC/ENOK, 'Voorgestelde rentekoersstruktuur vir leenings van die ENOK', (typescript, 1981, unpublished).
International Karakul Secretariat, *Study to Determine Possible Improvements to the Effectiveness of the Marketing of SWAKARA*, (report by the Battelle Research Centre, Geneva, 1981).
UK, Foreign Office, *South West Africa* (F.O. Handbook 112, 1920).
USAID, *Namibia: anticipation of economic and humanitarian needs,*

(Washington, 1976).
USAID/SADAP, *Namibia: a Report to the Congress on Development Needs and Opportunities for Cooperation in Southern Africa*, (Washington, 1979).
Constitutional Conference of SWA *Ontwikkelingspotensiaal van SWA: eerste verslag van die veerde komitee van die Staatkundige Beraad*, (SWA Advisory Planning Dept., Windhoek, 1977, unpublished).

(c) Publications and statements

SA, Dept of Agriculture, Information leaflets on karakul farming, (extracts from the official monthly *Farming in South Africa*, (1979-80).
SA, Dept of Bantu Admin. and Development, Ethnological studies series: districts of Okahandja, Otjiwarongo, Omaruru, Karibib, Windhoek (unpublished), Gobabis, Grootfontein, (Pretoria, 1951-8).
SA, Dept of Foreign Affairs, *SWA Survey 1967, SWA Survey 1974*.
SA, Dept of Foreign Affairs, *Owambo* (1971).
SA Minister of Water Affairs 'Water for SWA', (transcript of speech to National Party Congress, Windhoek, 23/7/74).
SWA Admin., Division of Nature Conservation, *The farmer and his game*, (Windhoek, 1977).
SWA Admin., Division of Nature Conservation, *Nature Conservation Legislation* (Windhoek 1978).
SWA/Namibia, Administrator-General, *SWA/Namibia Survey*. (Press Office, Windhoek, 1980).
SWA, Administrator General, Economic Advisory Committee, *The Economy of SWA/Namibia*, (report 1978, published Windhoek, 1980).
SWA/Namibia, Directorate of Water Affairs, *25 years of water supply to SWA, 1954-79*, (Windhoek, 1980).
FNDC/ENOK, *Investment in SWA/Namibia* (Windhoek, ?1980).
SA, Dept. of Agriculture/SA Railways & Harbours, *SWA: Particulars Concerning Land Settlement*, (Pretoria, 1923).